Andy Pardoe is a leading AI thought leader, consultant, speaker and author. He is the Founder and CEO of the Wisdom Works Group consultancy and is also the Managing Partner of Wisdom Works Ventures, a specialist accelerator for AI start-ups. He is the Chair of the Deep Tech Innovation Centre at the University of Warwick.

Confident AI

*The essential skills for working
with artificial intelligence*

Andy Pardoe

KoganPage

Publisher's note
Every possible effort has been made to ensure that the information contained in this book is accurate at the time of going to press, and the publishers and authors cannot accept responsibility for any errors or omissions, however caused. No responsibility for loss or damage occasioned to any person acting, or refraining from action, as a result of the material in this publication can be accepted by the editor, the publisher or the author.

First published in Great Britain and the United States in 2024 by Kogan Page Limited

2nd Floor, 45 Gee Street
London
EC1V 3RS
United Kingdom

8 W 38th Street, Suite 902
New York, NY 10018
USA

www.koganpage.com

Kogan Page books are printed on paper from sustainable forests.

ISBNs

Hardback	978 1 3986 1620 2
Paperback	978 1 3986 1572 4
Ebook	978 1 3986 1621 9

British Library Cataloguing-in-Publication Data
A CIP record for this book is available from the British Library.

Library of Congress Control Number
202398615724

Typeset by Integra Software Services, Pondicherry
Print production managed by Jellyfish
Printed and bound by CPI Group (UK) Ltd, Croydon, CR0 4YY

To my parents and wife – for always being there for me.

Contents

List of figures xiii
About the author xiv
Bonus for readers xvi
Preface xvii
Acknowledgements xx
List of abbreviations xxi

Introduction 1

PART ONE
Why AI? 13

01 Why work in AI? 15
   The researcher 18
   The data scientist 19
   The head of data science 20
   Other technical roles 20
   Senior roles 22
   New roles 23
   Other key skills and capabilities 24
   The five success factors for AI 28
   Fast-forward 10 years 31
   Why not work in AI? 32
   Notes 33

02 AI myths 34
   Myth 1: AI is just a fad that will soon fade away 36
   Myth 2: Only big businesses can afford AI 37
   Myth 3: Machines will soon replace humans in the
      workforce 38

Myth 4: AI is too difficult to implement 39
Myth 5: AI will never be able to replicate human
    levels of intelligence 40
Myth 6: You need to be a technologist to work
    in the field of AI 41
Myth 7: Building AI will become fully automated 43
Myth 8: AI is Infallible and always right 45
Other myths 46
Future AI myths 47
Myth busting 49
Notes 50

03   Applications of AI 51
Healthcare 53
Finance 54
Sales and marketing 55
Education 56
Industry and manufacturing 56
Agriculture and environmental monitoring 57
Entertainment and creative industries 58
Energy and utilities 58
Government and public services 59
Legal and compliance 60
Supply chain and logistics 60
Human resources and talent management 61
Non-profit and social impact 62
Emerging and cross-industry applications 62
Deep tech 63
Final thoughts 63
Notes 64

04   A future perspective 66
Emerging trends in AI 69
Ethical and societal considerations 70

The evolution of AI careers 72
Research and innovation 73
The future of work 75
Challenges and uncertainties 75
Final thoughts – the road ahead 80
Notes 81

PART TWO
The technology 83

05 Understanding AI 85
Overview 85
The history of AI 86
Innovation at the speed of thought 89
Overview of AI 90
The beauty of intelligence and the human brain 93
Artificial general intelligence 94
Superintelligence and the singularity 95
Measuring intelligence 96
Recent advances 97
Final thoughts 99

06 Overview of machine learning 101
The basics of machine learning 101
Learning approaches 108
Final thoughts 111

07 Data and infrastructure 113
Data foundations 114
Technical infrastructure and architecture 118
Final thoughts 122

08 Advanced topics 124
Deep learning 124
Natural language 125
Video and image analytics 126
Generative algorithms 126
The data science toolbox 129
Distributed computing 134
Quantum computing 134
Data privacy and trust 135
Regulation 137
A new era of computing – generative waves 137
Final thoughts 141

PART THREE
The process 143

09 Elements of an AI strategy 145
The nine elements of an AI strategy 147
One: Strategy alignment and business need 147
Two: AI roadmap 149
Three: Technical infrastructure and data foundations 149
Four: Data science frameworks 151
Five: Skills and talent 153
Six: Culture of innovation 158
Seven: Organizational structure and governance 160
Eight: Planning, vendors and partners 164
Nine: Managing an AI-powered workforce 166
Final thoughts 171
Note 172

10 Implementing AI 173
12 challenges of AI adoption 174
Overcoming implementation challenges 175
Implementation approaches 176
Internal AI development 177

AI consultancies 178
Vendor products and services 179
The hybrid approach 180
Final thoughts 181

11 Governance, ethics and safety 182
Governance 183
Ethics 184
Safety 186
Core AI principles 187
AI governance management 199
Final thoughts 201
Note 201

PART FOUR
The people 203

12 People: key characteristics 205
Key characteristics of a data scientist 206
Problem solving 206
Communication skills 207
Teamwork, office politics and personalities 208
Community support 209
Final thoughts 210

13 Different teams and roles 212
Data science pods 213
Pod roles 213
Supporting roles 214
Other roles (outside of the pods) 215
Other stakeholders 216
Communities of practice 217
Organizational structure 218
Final thoughts 219

14 Getting started 220
   Students and first job 221
   Professionals and career change 223
   Other considerations 224
   Final thoughts 225

15 Career development 226
   The AI career landscape 227
   Understanding AI career paths 229
   AI career options 230
   Building a strong foundation 232
   Gaining practical experience 233
   Networking and mentorship 234
   Staying informed and adapting 235
   Landing your first AI job 236
   Career advancement and growth 236
   Your AI career journey starts now 238
   Final thoughts 239
   Notes 239

Conclusion 240
The technology 241
The process and the people 242
Four key takeaways 243
Summary 245
Epilogue 246

Appendix 248
Index 266

List of figures

Figure 3.1   The 10 stages of AI adoption 52
Figure 7.1   Data layers with analytics, AI and
              automation 115
Figure 7.2   360 customer view 116
Figure 7.3   Data as a service capabilities 117
Figure 9.1   The nine elements of an AI strategy 146
Figure 9.2   The data science framework 153
Figure 9.3   Data science framework: four focus areas 154
Figure 9.4   Data science pipeline/workflow 155
Figure 9.5   Operating model structures ordered by adoption
              maturity 161
Figure 11.1   Example set of AI core principles 188

About the author

Professor Andy Pardoe has a lifelong interest in computer science and artificial intelligence (AI).

This obsession started in his very early teens, hearing for the first time on television about biologically inspired computing, and from that point on being singularly motivated to learn more about technical implementations of intelligence that replicated the way our own biological computational unit (our brain) worked. He studied Computer Systems Engineering at Warwick University and continued on to do a PhD in AI, specifically neural networks.

He was previously the Principal Director for Artificial Intelligence at Accenture Digital with a focus on delivery across multiple industry groups including Financial Services, Health and Public Safety, and Telecommunications, Media and High Technology, also specializing in AI Innovation and Strategy aligned to demonstrating potential applications helping to increase adoption and commercialization.

Currently Andy leads an AI consultancy, advising SMEs and PLCs on their adoption of AI capabilities to improve their business processes, products and services. The ventures consultancy advises many AI start-up companies, providing a range of support, both business and technical. Many of the AI start-up founders he advises have PhDs in Machine Learning and are looking to develop new AI innovations as part of their product offering.

Andy is also the chair of the Deep Tech Innovation Centre, part of the Warwick Innovation District at the University of Warwick, helping Deep Tech founders to commercialize their research and accelerate the early stages of these tech start-ups.

Andy is a board advisor to several companies, helping them to identify the strategic advantages of utilizing AI across the value chain, including integrating AI-powered functionality within current and new products and services.

An international keynote speaker, author, thought leader and futurist on the topic of artificial intelligence, in 2017 he was listed by IBM Watson as one of the Top 30 AI Influencers globally. Andy is credited as an expert advisor to the AI film documentary, *We Need to Talk about AI*, released by Universal Pictures in 2020. He is the co-author of *The AI Book* and *60 Leaders in AI*, and has published the books *AI Strategy for Business Leaders* and *IQ Unknown*, on how AI is changing the world.

Bonus for readers

Thanks for choosing this book to read. You have made a big first step towards your new career in the world of artificial intelligence.

To further support your initial steps into the world of AI, all readers can gain access to my free resource which has a collection of articles and insights on the topic of AI and is updated regularly. Just visit Informed.AI to learn more.

I have also created a dedicated set of resources specifically to accompany this book, which is available at itsallonesandzeros.com/confidentAI

You can also visit my main website at Pardoe.AI to learn more about me and the work that I do.

Happy reading and good luck as you start your career in the wonderful field of AI.

Preface

The field of artificial intelligence (AI) started way back in the 1950s, but it is only in the last 20 years or so that the interest in AI has become much more mainstream. There are many reasons for this recent explosion of curiosity in the topic which is now leading to widespread utilization of AI and machine learning (ML) across a multitude of industries and applications.

Certainly, the capabilities of AI and ML have improving significantly with advances such as deep learning (DL) and reinforcement learning (RL) over the last decade or so, with many narrow applications having been demonstrated to deliver performance equivalent to human levels of ability. Deep learning algorithms and architectures set the groundwork on which much of the recent progress has been made and certainly form the foundation for the popular generative AI applications we see today.

Supporting the advances in deep learning are three core enabling technologies facilitating the rapid rise of AI applications and systems. The first is big data platforms, which have made it a lot easier to capture, store and manage data – giving us huge quantities of information that can be used as training data in machine learning models. The second is the move towards cloud computing, making it easier to gain access to computation resources at a fraction of the cost of owning the underlying hardware outright. The third happened almost by accident. The graphics cards for gaming computers required significant parallel processing – this feature was perfectly aligned to running the training of neural networks and provided major time acceleration due to the ability to divide the processing across many cores within a single GPU. It is the combination of these three enabling technologies that provides the foundation for many of the most recent advances in the world of AI.

In 2023, we saw another significant advancement that created huge interest in AI. The fusion of generative AI and conversational AI produced the first application driven by general-purpose AI (GPAI), which saw over 100 million users sign up to use it within two months of its release – the fastest customer onboarding for any technology product ever. The possibilities of this new capability created huge excitement and opened the eyes of many people to the true potential of artificial intelligence.

With many commentators expressing an exponential increase in technical innovation right now, the AI industry and the field of AI research have been advancing at an unprecedented pace in recent months. With the big technology firms such as Microsoft, Google, Amazon, IBM and Meta keen to get first-mover advantage for their users, it makes it a very dynamic and competitive environment for the entire AI ecosystem of vendors, consultancies and start-ups. There is significant opportunity for new AI-powered products and services.

The world is becoming more dependent on and impacted by technology and in particular AI-driven systems. This means that the future of work is going to be influenced and affected by AI-enabled technologies – so much so that the workforce of the future will need to understand how to use AI tools and applications to give them a productivity edge they will need to compete.

Therefore, having confidence with AI technology, applications, tools and capabilities will be a major benefit to everyone, both professionally and personally. Understanding what AI can do, how it does it, its limitations and opportunities, will be the way you can advance your career and keep yourself ahead in the workplace.

This applies to not only those who want to work in the field of AI to help build new machine learning applications, but to everyone, as AI will become a core tool in the workplace for every role across every industry. Those who master the use of AI in their jobs will have a significant advantage over those who are less knowledgeable about the AI-driven tools and applications available. We are all going to be augmented and amplified by the abilities of AI technologies if we know how to best use them for our benefit.

The future of work is going to look very different from today, with the potential for us all to be empowered with AI-based digital assistants, automating the mundane and doing the heavy lifting on simple and repetitive tasks. Those who embrace this new future quickly will have a significant advantage, with super-human productivity and abilities that those without this type of support will struggle with.

Acknowledgements

I would like to thank my very understanding wife Jennifer for all her support and encouragement during the process of writing this book. Writing requires a lot of time and therefore many early mornings, late evenings, weekends and holidays have been sacrificed to create this book.

To the thousands of AI researchers and academics around the world that have moved the field of AI so far forward over the last few decades, years and months, I thank you for your dedication to the field and determination to move us towards the moonshot of artificial general intelligence. I also wish to recognize the professionals and researchers that bring a more cautionary and controlled perspective on the technology, to help reduce some of the hype we see with every new development and highlight some of the risks and ethical concerns that must be addressed as we progress forward. We must move forward with a responsible and trustworthy approach to benefit all.

I would also like to thank the individuals and companies that have allowed me to share their stories within the case studies of this book. It was important to me to use real-life examples from firms that are on the cutting edge of AI innovation and that I know personally.

My thanks also go to Kogan Page publishers and in particular Matt James for his continued support and guidance throughout the development of this book. His insights and editing of my initial drafts have been an invaluable help.

And finally, to my wonderful network of supporters, who always provide me with so much motivation and inspiration.

List of abbreviations

AGI:	Artificial General Intelligence
AI:	Artificial Intelligence
API:	Application Programming Interface
AWS:	Amazon Web Services
CAIO:	Chief AI Officer
CDO:	Chief Data Officer
CIO:	Chief Information Officer
CoE:	Centre of Excellence (for organization of data science teams)
CoP:	Community of Practice
CTO:	Chief Technology Officer
DaaS:	Data as a Service
DL:	Deep Learning
FPGA:	Field Programmable Gate Arrays
GCP:	Google Cloud Platform
GPAI:	General-Purpose AI
GPU:	Graphical Processing Unit
IPA:	Intelligent Process Automation
LLM:	Large Language Model
ML:	Machine Learning
MLOps:	Machine Learning Operations
RL:	Reinforcement Learning
ROI:	Return on Investment
RPA:	Robotic Process Automation
SDLC:	Software Development Lifecycle
STEM:	Science, Technology, Engineering and Mathematics

Introduction

The world is changing, and fast. Much faster than ever before, and at such a rate that it is becoming difficult to keep up with the various advancements. Unlike previous industrial revolutions, we see advancements occurring in many different industries. Some say this rate of change is exponential, but it actually feels faster than that.[1]

Technology is driving much of this transformation, enabling us to increase productivity, make better-informed decisions and solve many problems we have previously struggled with. Artificial intelligence is having a significant impact on every industry and every aspect of business and the workplace. It is probably the most disruptive technology we will ever see, likely to change our world in ways we have yet to imagine.

We experienced a real pivotal moment in 2023, with the first general-purpose AI having mass-market appeal based on its range of applications and utility. The world woke up to the potential of AI and its widespread impact. It's true to say that AI has come of age, found its utility and demonstrated mass application that can be used by individuals and businesses of all sizes and industries. The technology industry moved fast to integrate the core elements and then to adapt and extend its capabilities to realize its full potential for all.

This ultimately means more roles within the workplace will need to leverage AI capabilities as part of their work. Understanding and using AI will become an essential skill in the workplace. In the future we will all need to be confident with AI and not just in the workplace; it will play a significant part in our personal lives too.

It is clear that every role in every industry will be augmented with a range of AI tools and applications, and many people will benefit from AI-powered digital assistants that will be supporting us in our work, automating tasks, performing mundane work and freeing humans to focus on the more complex, creative and difficult jobs that need to be done. Using AI to do the jobs that are easy to automate will give us more time to deal with the more challenging activities.

As technology and AI continues at pace to change our world, we all need to gain more understanding of what it is and how it works, to allow us to maximize the benefits and productivity gains from its application. We need to educate ourselves about the strengths and weaknesses of the technology, understanding the challenges and opportunities it presents.

Certainly, with the introduction of ChatGPT[2] in November 2022, the applications of AI, and in particular the combination of generative and conversational AI, rapidly became mainstream, with over 100 million users of the tool from OpenAI within a couple of months.[3] This was the first widely used general-purpose AI, able to do a wide range of tasks, from creating poems to writing programming code. A tool that anyone can use for a multitude of tasks, its utility seems endless, and now the potential of AI is boundless.

The tech industry took generative AI and ran with it at speed in 2023, extending and enhancing the capabilities of ChatGPT with co-pilots and grounding, plugins and refinements; the tech industry has never produced so much so fast as it did in the year.

It wasn't just the big tech firms either; we saw a significant rise in generative AI start-ups and established firms building upon the foundations.

This has changed the game for everyone. Professional services and consulting firms have also needed to adjust their strategies, with many investing heavily to capture some expertise and capabilities to provide to their clients. Other businesses have needed to alter their business models, products and services to adjust to this new normal of digital assistants and easy productivity gains.

We will look back at 2023 as a major milestone for the adoption of AI, with many companies, who had previously taken little notice of the capabilities of AI, now seriously looking to apply AI across their business. The management teams of businesses of all sizes and industries are waking up to the innovation and disruption that AI is bringing into the environment. This will generate more opportunities for those who have the skills and knowledge to work with AI, changing the environment of the workforce much more than the fax machine, typewriter or personal computer ever did.

Overview

The field of artificial intelligence is complex and, in many ways, still in its infancy. While the term was coined back in the 1950s, only in this last few decades have we started to see major breakthroughs that have allowed us to build useful tools and applications that have started to solve some challenging problems for us.

Technology in general is maturing fast, with many experts claiming the rate of change is now exponential. We saw this firsthand in 2023, with the big tech firms launching their own versions of generative AI, together with open-source variations of the large language models (LLMs), integrations into many different products and the evolution of co-pilots allowing others to more easily leverage the technology and apply it to many different problems.

For the first time in our history, a general-purpose AI (GPAI) has achieved mainstream market share and, more importantly than that, it has sparked the imagination of millions of people about the endless possibilities of AI-powered applications. Therefore, it is the perfect time to have a career in AI, as companies of all sizes and across most industries are paying real attention to how AI could benefit their business objectives, create competitive advantage and deliver productivity gains. It's another innovation cycle (known as the S-curve of innovation), and a race against your competitors to capture the benefits of AI. There will be winners and losers in this fast-moving dynamic environment. We see this already with the competition between the big tech firms, each attempting to stamp their authority, expertise and leadership, with rapid releases of their own AI-based models and tools.

A golden age of the algorithm

It seems obvious that the future of wealth and prosperity will be driven by expertise with advanced algorithms. Some call it the next space race, others the next arms race, but either way, we are entering the golden age of the algorithm. This is not only a national race, but a commercial and individual race too.

We have already heard about an AI fighter pilot[4] that is more performant and capable than the best of the best human test pilots, and AI applications that are helping to defend against security cyber-attacks. Computers are hacking computers. How is this not digital warfare?

But this isn't just about traditional warfare; this is about business and commercial success too. Only those companies that embrace the benefits that advanced algorithms can deliver will survive. This will be the new major differentiator for firms. One only has to look at some of the trailblazing firms to already see this happening. Business models are changing, dramatically, with global start-ups, unicorns, having defined the landscape of many traditional businesses.

Algorithms will have a massive impact on individuals too. In many cases they already are, from mortgage approvals, medical diagnosis and recommendations for purchases to who you should date, they touch our lives in so many different and usually hidden ways that one can argue we are already being shaped and controlled by the power of the algorithm. We do this as we trust that data holds the universal truth and that we are making better decisions by putting our faith in the algorithms that analyse these huge datasets.

This raises a lot of questions around AI ethics, AI governance and AI safety. These are hot topics and many high-profile advocates are highlighting a need for more investment and research on these subjects to support the rise of AI in general. Without these support frameworks the algorithms could spin out of control.

The truth about (intelligent) automation

The truth is that automation capabilities across all industries have been developing for a very long time, but only now are we starting to see the major impact of such complete automation.

From the use of horses to help plough fields, to tractors and finally to the robo-crop that automatically removes weeds on fields – take any industry and you can find examples, from the first industrial revolution to this one, of automation slowly becoming more powerful, more complete and more transformative.

What is different this time is that we can see real possibilities of complete and total automation, even with tasks and jobs that we might have thought would be impossible to automate only a few years ago. This is driven by the power of the algorithm and specifically machine learning capabilities that have significantly advanced over the last five years.

Here we see a fusion of automation techniques with machine learning to augment the automation with intelligent decision making. This lack of intelligence from automation has been the bottleneck holding back our ability to fully automate complete processes.

Automation also comes in different guises, from software automation (often referred to as robotic process automation), to manufacturing automation (the production line), to humanoid robotics (androids) that can be multi-purpose in their function.

One of the ways companies look to introduce AI and machine learning is to add intelligence into their software automations, turning robotic process automation (RPA) into intelligent process automation (IPA).

We should not be scared of this – it is just the next step in our evolution. We should embrace it and help figure out what this means for humankind – the potential of this automation is beyond our wildest dreams. In saying this, I do not want to overlook the potential negative impact on some roles and industries; like any industrial revolution or disruptive technology, there will be challenges for us to overcome, but how we manage this at a national and global scale will be key to our success.

Personally, I am looking forward to having my work augmented with smart automated machines that allow me to free up some of my time to focus on more interesting challenges. My hope is that many of us can embrace the changes in the same way.

A short history of AI

The history of artificial intelligence can be traced back to the 1950s when researchers first began exploring the idea of creating machines that could perform tasks that would normally require human intelligence. The Dartmouth Conference in 1956 is widely considered the birthplace of AI. Researchers gathered to discuss the possibility of building machines that could perform tasks that normally require human intelligence, such as understanding natural language, recognizing objects and solving problems.

In the 1960s the first AI programs were developed, including John McCarthy's Logic Theorist and Herbert Simon's General Problem Solver. These programs were able to perform simple tasks, such as solving mathematical problems, playing games and translating languages.

However, in 1966 the first AI winter (a term used to indicate a period of cooling off or slowdown in the AI industry) began as a result of overstated expectations and underfunding. Despite the early successes, researchers were unable to develop machines that could perform more complex tasks, leading to a decrease in funding and a slowdown in progress.

Then in the 1970s, AI experienced a resurgence, with the development of expert systems able to perform specific tasks that normally require human expertise, such as diagnosing diseases, recommending treatments and making financial predictions.

Our second AI winter began in the late 1980s due to a combination of overstated expectations and the lack of progress in developing truly intelligent machines. Funding for AI research decreased, and many researchers left the field.

In the mid to late '90s, we experienced another resurgence, with the development of machine learning algorithms, such as decision trees, neural networks and support vector machines, which allowed machines to learn from data and improve their performance over time.

Then in 1997, a chess match between Deep Blue and Garry Kasparov took place, with Deep Blue, an AI system developed by IBM, defeating the world chess champion. This marked a significant milestone in the development of AI, demonstrating the ability of machines to perform tasks that require human-level intelligence.

This started another wave of enthusiasm in the 2010s, with the advance of deep learning algorithms, which allowed machines to learn and make predictions based on large amounts of data. These algorithms have been used to achieve state-of-the-art results in tasks such as image and speech recognition, natural language processing and autonomous driving – and are able for the first time in our history to show performance better than humans at specific tasks.

DeepMind, a UK-based AI company now owned by Google, showcased a number of applications, including AlphaGo[5] and AlphaFold,[6] which leveraged new techniques such as reinforcement learning and produced stunning results demonstrating the true potential of AI to the world.

And at the end of 2022, OpenAI amazed the world with its ChatGPT tool, making the whole AI industry and the wider tech industry focus on generative and conversational AI and integrating the technology into other tools and products. While the hype surrounding this new AI ability was intense, and it obviously had some issues (hallucinations, data leakage, data privacy and trust), it has made AI mainstream and opened the eyes of many CEOs to the possibilities it can provide.

There is also an increasing focus on AI safety, responsibility, ethics and governance, which will open more career opportunities and roles in the near future. The UK hosted the first global AI Safety Summit towards the end of 2023, to encourage leaders from countries across the world to come together and agree to oversee the responsible creation of frontier models.

Today, AI is being used in a wide range of applications, from healthcare to finance, and is playing an increasingly important role in our daily lives. Despite this progress, the development of truly intelligent machines remains a challenge, and AI continues to be an active area of research and development.

The essential skills for working with AI

There are a multitude of options for working in the field of AI, and while some will require technical knowledge and a computer science background, many others will require different skills and experience, opening up opportunities for countless people to work in the AI sector.

You might be a student working towards an MSc in machine learning or artificial intelligence, aiming for a career either in academic research or to work within a data science team building AI and machine learning solutions for your employer or client.

The demand for those with skills in AI and machine learning is at an all-time high, and only looks to increase in the next few years as more and more businesses look to adopt these technologies into their own environment and embed them into their products and services. It is estimated that the global demand for data scientists will increase by 11.5 million by 2026.[7]

You may be a technologist already working with more traditional programming languages and technologies, but looking to retrain as a data scientist or ML Ops engineer. Here there are various educational and training opportunities available to you, with many free resources for basic training to get you started.

There is also increasing demand for middle and senior management to learn more about AI, to understand how it works and what it can do. Again, there is a huge amount of information available online and various workshops and training sessions can be arranged for more personal and tailored education.

However, beyond these classic career paths, there are many other ways in which you might work with AI in your job. You might be part of the technology department of a company, but not directly building the AI being used – for example, you might be the compliance officer, or a business analyst, or one of the testing team. Roles across the organization will be users of AI too, from the sales and marketing teams to human resources, finance, operations, legal and many others.

This is before considering all the new roles that are slowly coming into the workplace; we have recently seen the rise of the role of prompt engineer with generative AI, for example. This is a non-technical role in which people help to get the best output from these tools by making changes to the input provided.

Finally, we are all consumers of applications and tools that are starting to use AI to provide additional intelligent and personalized functionality.

All of these different roles, career paths and ways we interact with the technology will determine the specific skills and knowledge we need to maximize our productivity leveraging AI. We will explore these different career paths and the various skills needed to excel at them.

You may be reading this, thinking that you need to have a deep understanding of technology or artificial intelligence in order to leverage the technology. This is certainly not the case, and as you read this book, you will understand that many different types of skills, experience and knowledge will be valued and beneficial to those looking to get the most out of AI technologies in the workplace.

Book structure

The book is divided into four parts. The first part looks to set the scene and discusses why AI is now so important and why you should consider a career in AI. The following three parts focus on the Technology, the Process and the People. These are key areas to understand when working in AI, as it's not just about the technology. The people involved and the process we follow are key to the long-term success of our application of AI.

For the majority of my career in technology, I have appreciated that working in a technology department within a company requires as much focus on the people and process as it does the technology. As a leader in IT, you have to be focused on all three areas to be successful. Without the people, nothing happens, without the process things can go wrong and without the right technology we will fail to deliver the product or service needed. This is why the book covers all three aspects, as without consideration of all three, any technology change is at risk of failure.

Throughout the book, I will provide references to and examples of key tools and frameworks, as well as case studies and insights into real-world experiences that will help to illustrate and support the relevant topic of discussion. I will also give a few career tips that I have learnt along my career that might also serve you well in yours.

Notes

1 While exponential growth is quoted to explain that technology is moving at an incredible rate, there are rates of growth that are even faster than exponential, en.wikipedia.org/wiki/Double_exponential_function (archived at https://perma.cc/388N-5B9G)

2 ChatGPT, en.wikipedia.org/wiki/ChatGPT (archived at https://perma.cc/Z69W-ABDN)

3 Hu, K (2023) ChatGPT sets record for fastest-growing user base – analyst note, *Reuters*, www.reuters.com/technology/chatgpt-sets-record-fastest-growing-user-base-analyst-note-2023-02-01 (archived at https://perma.cc/HLM2-AGZK)

4 Walsh, A (2023) AI-powered pilot dominates human rival in aerial dogfight, *Flying*, www.flyingmag.com/aipowered-pilot-dominates-human-rival-in-aerial-dogfight (archived at https://perma.cc/JD66-VGTK)

5 DeepMind AlphaGo, deepmind.google/technologies/alphago/ (archived at https://perma.cc/LJ8H-JTLJ)

6 DeepMind AlphaFold, deepmind.google/technologies/alphafold/ (archived at https://perma.cc/K3SV-AN77)

7 United States Data Science Institute (nd) Data science: unlocking careers for the future, www.usdsi.org/data-science-insights/unlocking-careers-for-the-future (archived at https://perma.cc/C5D6-BMUH)

PART ONE

Why AI?

It might be easy to think that AI is just the next technology trend, here today and gone tomorrow, replaced with the next new programming language, platform, application or architectural design. While we have seen this continued innovation and renewal with many other forms of technology, with artificial intelligence it's a very different situation. After all, AI is already constantly reinventing itself; the best and latest techniques today are much more advanced than what was cutting edge in the world of AI 10 years ago, and given the rate of change we are seeing, the AI of the near future will be very different to what we have right now.

This makes the field of AI the most important and interesting area of technology, as it is concerned with building solutions using the latest advances in technology we have at any point in time. I like to think about AI as just being the most advanced technology available, with the technology now very much focused on replicating intelligent behaviour.

There simply isn't a better time to start your career in AI, as the recent developments in generative AI have made it a mass-market technology with adoption happening across industries and with businesses of all sizes.

The profession of AI and machine learning (often referred to as data science) has also matured significantly over the last few years, with many tools, frameworks and platforms to support the process and workflow of developing and deploying machine learning models.

The field of AI is in many ways still in its infancy but over the last few years it has matured and become much more of a profession. We need this to continue to ensure all the risks and challenges are properly dealt with by experienced and knowledgeable people who can bring diverse thinking and a robust approach to adoption.

CHAPTER ONE

Why work in AI?

The future of work is now with us. The Covid-19 pandemic has dramatically helped to accelerate digital transformation, with online retail and remote working becoming important for the survival of many businesses, and even the acceleration of AI-based chatbots for customer support, as client services staff had to work from home and in some cases struggled with remote access. With Microsoft describing it as *2 years of digital transformation in 2 months*,[1] this acceleration of digital transformation opened the door to increased adoption of AI technologies as well.

We are all having to adapt to a technology-first environment by becoming digital natives. Obviously, there will be some industries and roles that have little if any use for AI, but as the world continues to rely more on technology-powered commerce we will see the need for increased education, skills and training to support the changing landscape of the workplace.

Technology is an enabler, helping businesses to achieve objectives more efficiently and more accurately. Since the very first machine code programs and mainframe computers, the abilities of technology have increased at pace over the decades. While the field of artificial intelligence was born in the 1950s, it is only over the last 20 years or so that we have really seen widespread adoption and acceptance of AI-powered applications and systems.

Despite this 70-year heritage, the AI industry is still relatively new, partly because what AI is keeps changing and the research and developments are happening now at a blistering rate, some might say exponential. A prime example of this rapid change is the term and role of data scientist. This term is relatively new in general usage; although it was first coined in the 1960s/1970s it was only first referenced at conferences in the late 1990s.[2] We will talk more about the role of data scientist later in this chapter, but for now it is enough to demonstrate the constantly changing face of AI, with new algorithms, hardware, training models and job roles.

We also see how the profession of AI is becoming increasingly more mature, with more emphasis on taking a thorough and robust approach. The tools, frameworks and platforms have also matured in recent years to provide the supporting infrastructure to facilitate a more professional outcome. This is compounded by the requirements from regulators and companies' internal governance processes to ensure ethical and trustworthy implementations of AI applications and systems. This new level of professionalism will help to control the rush for innovation and competitive advantage, which will inevitably cause some shortcomings and failures.

Certainly, the world of AI is now mainstream. The general-purpose application of generative AI has woken the business world up to its various possibilities and benefits across the business value chain, from sales and marketing and customer support to back-office operations and transactional processing.

So, to ask the question, why would any young person new to the workplace, or those professionals looking for a career change, want to work in the field of AI? We might argue that the field is too complex and dynamic, and therefore it's too risky to commit to a career in AI. The counterargument is that the field of AI is the ultimate advancement of technology, and the fact that it is such a complex and dynamic environment now means that there are plenty of opportunities to foster a brilliant career – plenty of space in the field of AI to become a leader and expert, and lots of innovations yet to happen with significant room for career growth and commercial exploitation. It's a vast landscape of opportunity.

There is also a natural tendency to assume that to work in technology one needs to be technical. This is certainly not the case. Many people I know who work in technology didn't study it at school or university, and only moved into the area of technology once they started working. However, those that did work in the technology area had the curiosity to learn about it and dedicated time to become knowledgeable.

There are many different career paths, with numerous roles requiring a range of skills and aptitudes – there is a world of possibilities for anyone interested in working in artificial intelligence.

People change jobs on average every three to five years, and often this would be a significant career change. I know of many experienced software developers who have decided to retrain as data scientists. Others move from IT into the business functions, and some change industries altogether. Moving companies, changing roles or even industries is possible, and many people do this over their careers. With the rapid pace of change in technology and business, it is almost impossible to not need to redefine oneself, growing with your knowledge and experience and seeking new opportunities where they arise.

However, despite the job market being relatively fluid, it is still a competitive market and so you need to give yourself the best possible chance of getting the job you desire. This applies to new graduates entering the job market for the first time, and also to those more experienced professionals who are looking to make a switch. Reading this book is a great first step towards your new career in AI, but you will need to invest more time to learn as much as possible to give yourself the best possible chance of success.

Let us explore the different career options for those wanting to get closer to the world of AI.

The researcher

The most academically aligned career would be that of AI researcher, helping to move the underlying methodologies, algorithms and architectures of AI and ML forward. While the world of AI is moving quickly, there is still a vast amount of research and development needed over the coming years. Many feel that generative AI has accelerated our progress towards AGI (artificial general intelligence), but we still have a long way to travel and many aspects of intelligence yet to master. Post-doc roles within universities are one path; many of the large technology firms also have dedicated research departments, but their goals will be more focused on applied AI for specific outcomes and applications, whereas universities are more open and less constrained.

The field of AI is also considerable, covering not just machine learning but many other important areas, including language understanding, knowledge representation, reasoning, planning, strategy, common sense and creativity to name a few. So, there are a range of research areas in which advancement and impact can be made. Ultimately, I believe that true advanced AI will be a combination of many approaches and methodologies coming together as a single consolidated technology.

While this choice of career is admirable and the demand for more research-capable AI developers will continue to grow, it is not for all, and there are many other levels of data scientist that can still contribute greatly to the field of AI without the need to create novel approaches that researchers strive to achieve.

The data scientist

A relatively new term in the world of AI, but fundamentally concerned with the application of AI and ML techniques to specific problems and datasets. There are different levels of experience and knowledge required for data scientists, depending on the requirements of the employment company. For example, if the task requires a novel solution to be created, this type of role is as much a researcher as it is an applied AI developer. For other, less complex tasks, it may be a simple activity to find an existing pre-trained model and tailor it to the specific dataset and task. Regardless of the level of complexity required, the role of data scientist is as much an art as a science, needing to use experience and knowledge to select the right type of technique and configure the architecture and parameters to optimize the output performance.

To be a successful data scientist, it is important to have a strong foundation in mathematics, statistics and computer science, as well as domain-specific knowledge and skills. Data scientists should also have strong problem-solving and communication skills and be able to work effectively in a team.

While mathematical, analytical and computer science skills are very important, communication skills are an essential part of the role too. While data visualization helps with this, a primary aspect of the data science role is being able to create the right narrative with the business implications of what the insights and model results are showing.

The role of data scientist is truly multi-disciplined, requiring a wide range of hard and soft skills to be performed well. This is why I am an advocate of data scientists having a broad foundation of knowledge and experience – this makes individuals who come from different areas and have various prior experiences strong candidates, but this is not mandatory.

While some data scientists will have some level of formal training and education, it is very possible for those already working in technology to retain and pivot towards a data science role.

The head of data science

Career progression as a data scientist would follow the normal path of becoming the senior and then lead data scientist within a team of others, and becoming the head of data science within a group or department.

Over time this may then open opportunities to become the head of data science for the entire company, and even gain the title of chief AI officer if the company felt the need for such a role at the board level.

As with any role leading a team of people, the required skills expand to people management as much as technical knowledge. These skills are often learnt over time with increasing team size and responsibilities. Often referred to as soft skills, they also include good communication skills (which you will have needed throughout the various data science roles), time management, and the ability to prioritize, delegate and navigate the organizational structure.

However, while it is most desirable for the head of data science to have a background in data science, it is possible for other technologists who have a good mix of technology and people management skills to take on such a position (and learn the details of data science on the job).

Other technical roles

There are many other roles within technology that support the development and implementation of AI, and are career options for those looking to move towards the area and get involved in projects that are building AI capabilities.

They include:

Data engineering: A role with responsibilities to manage and control data within the chosen platform(s). To help with data collection and processing pipelines to facilitate the tasks of the wider team.

ML engineering: Work on the scaling of AI deployments and implementing the mechanisms to make taking the models built by the data scientists to live production environments as easy as possible.

MLOps: Define, implement and manage the automated pipelines for data science development, testing, deployment, monitoring and maintenance. Support the data scientists with any additions or changes they need to the pipeline for specific models or tasks.

Data labeller: Support the data scientists with any data-labelling requirements for new or existing data.

ML trainers: Work on optimizing the configurations and hyper-parameters to create the best-performing ML models.

There are other technical roles that will support the AI teams with implementation, deployment and monitoring of AI systems and applications, including:

- architects
- product and user experience designers
- platform and infrastructure administrators
- database system administrators

Less technical roles will also be closely involved in the adoption of AI within an organization, including:

- product owners
- scrum masters
- business analysts

- project managers
- programme managers
- testers and QA (quality assurance) managers
- support teams and managers

As part of a sprint or Agile team, other roles including full-stack developers and UX designers might also get involved in projects building AI tools and applications.

Senior roles

There are also more senior roles that have some oversight and influence on the area of AI development and implementation, including:

- AI ethics manager or director – ensuring ethical, social and political perspectives are considered during the design, build and deployment of AI applications.
- Risk and compliance officer – responsible for the governance and management of risks within the business.
- Chief data officer – focused on the firm-wide governance and utility of data as an asset.
- Chief operations officer – responsible for the smooth operations of all systems and processes within the company, including the people and logistics.
- Chief information officer – responsible for all information systems within the enterprise.
- Chief technology officer – focused on all technology operations including the build of new systems and applications.

Each of these roles will have a mix of skills, knowledge and experience, but will not require the deep levels of AI technical background needed for more technical roles.

Fundamentally, each of our own career journeys is unique, each doing a range of different roles for various companies over time. Transitioning from one role to another, while it can be difficult, it is by no means impossible, and where there is a high demand and low supply, as there currently is in the field of AI, making that move is slightly easier than might otherwise be the case. A key element of shaping and directing your career is to let people know what you are looking to do; this will naturally create new career options.

New roles

The acceleration of AI is opening up opportunities for new roles at all levels within an organization, from chief AI officer to the latest emerging roles such as prompt engineer. As the field evolves over the coming years, we will most likely see even more roles being created, together with existing role changes in terms of the responsibilities and skills required.

Chief AI officer

Currently, only the largest of organizations would be able to benefit from a dedicated chief AI officer. For many smaller companies, they may only need a fractional CAIO role. The role has full oversight of all AI implementations across a business, defining and implementing the AI strategy, ensuring the right governance, audit and control are realized, all ethical considerations are factored into the working practices, and all appropriate AI policies are communicated to the entire workforce.

Prompt engineer

With the emergence of generative and conversational AI, the need to optimize the prompts provided to the LLM model to maximize the performance and get the best possible output from the tool meant that the technique of prompt engineering became increasingly important. It was easy to demonstrate how output results were improved by making the prompts more informative of the desired output with as much context as could be included. This has created the role of prompt engineer; however, this skill will eventually be absorbed by data scientists, and there may only be a limited number of dedicated prompt engineers over time. We simply do not know if this role will persist longer-term, or if it may even evolve, adding other similar skills into the role, for example, selection of training data for LLM model bespoke training.

Other key skills and capabilities

There are a variety of skills and capabilities key for succeeding in AI, from the more apparent mathematics and statistics to the less obvious communication skills and storytelling.

Mathematics and statistics

Data science involves the use of mathematics and statistics to extract insights and knowledge from data. There are many different mathematical and statistical concepts and techniques that are used in data science, and the specific concepts and techniques that are needed will depend on the specific goals and tasks of the project.

Some examples of mathematical and statistical concepts and techniques that are commonly used in data science include:

Linear algebra: A branch of mathematics that deals with linear equations and linear transformations. It is used in data science for tasks such as dimensionality reduction, matrix decomposition and principal component analysis. Some of the key concepts in linear algebra include vectors, matrices and linear transformations. Linear algebra is used in data science to represent and manipulate data in a structured and efficient way.

Calculus: A branch of mathematics that deals with the study of rates of change and the accumulation of quantities. It is used in data science for tasks such as optimization and gradient descent. Some of the key concepts in calculus include derivatives, integrals and limits. Calculus is used in data science to perform mathematical optimization and to understand the behaviour of machine learning models.

Probability: The study of random events and the likelihood of their occurrence. It is used in data science for tasks such as model evaluation, hypothesis testing and Bayesian inference. Some of the key concepts in probability include probability distributions, random variables and statistical independence. Probability is used in data science to analyse and understand the uncertainty and randomness inherent in data.

Statistics: A branch of mathematics that deals with the collection, analysis, interpretation, presentation and organization of data. It is used in data science for tasks such as data exploration, data visualization and statistical modelling. Some of the key concepts in statistics include descriptive statistics, statistical inference and statistical modelling. Statistics is used in data science to analyse and understand patterns and trends in data, and to draw conclusions and make predictions based on the data.

Getting started with programming

Programming is a fundamental skill for data scientists, as it allows them to work with data in a structured and automated way. There are several programming languages that are used in data science; two of the most popular are Python and R.

Python is a general-purpose programming language that is widely used in data science due to its large ecosystem of libraries and frameworks. It is a powerful language that is easy to learn, and it is used for tasks like data manipulation, visualization and machine learning.

R is a programming language specifically designed for statistical computing and data visualization. It is popular in the data science community due to its wide range of statistical and graphical functions, and its ability to handle large and complex datasets.

While it might be tempting to focus on the machine learning and model training aspects of these programming languages, having wider programming abilities, such as data management and processing, will serve you well in the longer term.

Big data and cloud

One of the enablers of deep learning was access to huge quantities of data. This was accomplished by the development of big data technologies that allowed data processing and analysis to be done on a scale that traditional database systems were unable to support. The improvements to scalable and parallel computing techniques allowed the vast data and processing needed to generate machine learning models based on considerable historical data repositories.

Having some knowledge of one or more of the cloud platforms and the various database technologies available will be very valuable, as a significant part of data science work is the management and manipulation of data to be used to train and test predictive models.

Data engineering

Data engineering is the practice of designing, building and maintaining the infrastructure and processes for storing, processing and analysing data. Data engineers are responsible for building and maintaining data pipelines, extract, transform and load (ETL) processes, and data storage and management systems.

While the amount of data collected and stored by firms has been increasing over the last few decades, the desire to now process and analyse this historical data has significantly escalated. This has developed the field of data engineering and produced new database technologies, tools and capabilities to support more real-time solutions, analytics and insights.

Data visualization

Data visualization is an important part of the data science process, as it allows you to explore and understand your data, communicate your findings to others, and identify patterns and trends. There are many advanced techniques and tools available for creating interactive and dynamic visualizations, such as dashboards and web-based plots.

Tools like D3.js, Matplotlib, Seaborn and Plotly allow you to create custom visualizations using JavaScript, and they provide a range of customization options and interactive features.

Data visualization is key to showing the business value of machine learning to business users. As a data scientist, you will need to understand what the insights from the model are telling you and then create the appropriate narrative to tell the story to the users. Visual representations of the insights provide dramatic context, so honing your abilities with building data visualizations will be a key skill.

Communication and storytelling

Communication and storytelling are important for a data scientist because they help to convey the insights and findings from data analysis to a wider audience. A data scientist may work with a wide range of stakeholders, including other data scientists, business leaders and technical experts, and it is important to be able to communicate effectively with these different groups. In order to do this, a data scientist may need to use a variety of communication methods and techniques, such as writing reports, presenting findings in meetings or conferences, and creating visualizations and other types of data-driven content.

Storytelling is particularly important for a data scientist because it helps to make complex data and analysis more accessible and understandable to a non-technical audience. By framing data and insights in the context of a story or narrative, a data scientist can help to engage and inspire others and persuade them to take action based on the findings.

Overall, effective communication and storytelling are essential skills for a data scientist because they help to ensure that the value of data analysis is recognized and understood by others and that the insights and recommendations generated by the data are effectively implemented and adopted.

The five success factors for AI

Many industries, such as financial services and telecommunications, have always been significant users of the latest technological advances but have also helped to push, from an innovation perspective, the capabilities of the various technologies. Today is no different to the past few decades in this respect, apart from five very important success factors that are empowering a real acceleration of AI applications. These five success factors, if companies can get them right, will dramatically improve the potential benefits of AI adoption and allow firms to deploy AI at scale across all departments of an organization.

First, as part of the Fourth Industrial Revolution we are seeing technology advancement taking an exponential path of development. The technologies are improving at rapid pace, and many of the seemingly unrelated technologies are actually empowering and accelerating the application of machine learning. For example, the desire for better performance with graphics cards for improved high-resolution gaming is the perfect multi-processor architecture for acceleration of deep learning training. The promise of quantum computing also has the potential to dramatically reduce the time taken to train machine learning models.

Big data platforms have allowed the capture of more and richer data, the fuel for training algorithms, especially deep learning, which requires huge quantities of training examples. This rate of change is creating a challenge for all industries to keep up.

Second, producing applications that embed machine learning models is a very different process than the more traditional methods of developing applications. Previously, business requirements would be collected and turned into functional requirements that teams of developers would use as a guide to write the code that delivered these functional capabilities within either existing or new applications. With machine learning, the paradigm has shifted. The historical data previously captured by the existing systems is used to determine the functionality (model) of the machine learning algorithm. This is a leap of faith. It requires that good-quality data has been captured in the first place. It also requires analysis to ensure that data equality represents all groups in a fair and unbiased way. This is a huge topic at the moment and is referred to more generally as responsible AI or the ethics of AI. Finding or training people with the prerequisite set of skills and knowledge is another challenge that many industries are facing.

Third, moving from an innovation activity, with a few small proof-of-concept or proof-of-value models, to being able to have a scaled delivery capability across the organization, allowing the full lifecycle to be properly orchestrated, interacting with many stakeholders and business groups in a coordinated way that provides the correct governance and validation, is not a simple activity. It requires cultural and organizational platforms and framework considerations to make this happen. The few organizations that are at this stage of the AI adoption journey are realizing this is a non-trivial process, and some are still struggling to get scaled machine learning models delivered into production environments.

Fourth, training a machine learning model and deploying it into a production environment is not the end of the story.

Because the underlying nature of business changes over time, so does the data, and therefore the performance accuracy of any training model. This produces the need for constant monitoring of the model performance, and potential regular re-training on the most recent datasets. This could be quarterly, monthly, weekly, daily, or for some particular needs online/streaming (for every new piece of data, the model is retrained with that data included in the training dataset). This requires additional tasks and support for systems not needed before.

Finally, the rapid deployment of automation and augmentation of work is transforming the workplace. Termed the 'future of work', everyone's role is changing, with the mundane and repetitive tasks being taken over by robotic process automation (known as RPA). But where will this lead us? As AI and machine learning become increasingly more capable with cognitive computing tasks (like reading and understanding text and speech, understanding the emotional responses of customers, visually inspecting images and documents), they will have the ability to automate more complex tasks and workflows. This is putting businesses under pressure to redefine their processes and innovate what is possible.

These five significant changes to the way companies need to operate will no doubt create opportunities as firms transform to adopt these new technologies. Fundamentally, this is part of the digital transformation that all organizations and industries are embarking on at the moment. For the first time, customers are demanding a highly personalized omnichannel experience. This is creating the impetus to leverage advanced data analytics and to develop new digital products and services. Ultimately these value-add services create a more competitive and dynamic environment for firms, putting them under increased pressure to deliver. The race is on, and those who are able to embrace the new digital native customers will endeavour to prosper and survive this period of disruption.

Fast-forward 10 years

Technology is changing at an extraordinary rate. It is most likely that all jobs, across all industries, will be augmented by AI tools and applications. We are already seeing tools to help with computer programming. Some automation has already been developed for data scientists (for example AutoML[3]), which takes some of the guesswork out of selecting the right model and parameters (but in many ways this is like using a sledgehammer to crack an egg).

But it is not too far-fetched to suggest that in three to five years' time we will be talking with an AI assistant that will help us develop the ML models and computer applications we need.

The role of a data scientist may change, with the soft skills becoming more important in the future, providing guidance and oversight to the AI agents (and business users) to create models to achieve the goals required. Essentially the data science process will become more streamlined and efficient in the future.

On the research and innovation side, we have much more to devise before we achieve anything close to human levels of intelligence – most experts in the field believe it will be many more decades of work before we can create artificial general intelligence.

Certainly, computer science has moved towards building intelligent systems and applications, and there will be significant focus on expanding the capabilities of these advanced intelligence applications over the coming years. The role of data scientist will change over the next 10 years, but the demand for people who understand how to build intelligent systems will continue to grow.

Since the Covid-19 pandemic, we have seen the future of work significantly evolve, with huge digital transformations across many different industries. This will continue in the 2020s and beyond as we use more AI agents to augment our lives, both personal and professional. Data scientists will also leverage AI agents and tools to help them optimize the applications they build as the working environment for all programmers and data scientists advances in the coming years.

With increasing demand and advancing technology, the need for people who understand and can build these systems will continue to grow for many years. While the profession will mature and the level of complexity increase, people will still have a major role to play in the creation and evolution of intelligence applications and tools that benefit us all.

This significant advanced capability for building technology and AI systems will have a disruptive impact on many other industries, making the future for all look more like an episode of *Star Trek*. The ability to use technology to help us devise new products and services, which would have taken many years to develop without such acceleration, will disrupt industries, changing the workplace and the fundamental nature of work itself. Some industries will be impacted beyond recognition, with new entrants challenging established firms that decide not to innovate as quickly.

Why not work in AI?

Whether it's the start of your career in AI, or a major change to your career direction, it can feel very uncomfortable – essentially the fear of the unknown. However, you will soon realize that it's the career journey that is the most important and influential element of your future career options. You will become greater than the sum of all the roles and industries you have worked in over time. Essentially, it's the journey that makes you unique in the workplace.

Regardless of who you are or at what stage of your career, we are all learning and expanding our roles and responsibilities.

Those around you will most likely be supportive and encouraging on your unique career journey.

AI is the most important and exciting area of technology, and the most important advancement in human history – it is completely understandable that you would want to be a contributor to this major milestone in human evolution. Building a completely new form of intelligence to rival our own is no small task, and we will need as many people as possible to help achieve it.

It could be considered the grand challenge to rival them all – the most important technology innovation we will ever build. The next step in our evolutionary development, no other intelligence has been able to replicate intelligent behaviour in an artificial form.

In this chapter I have given you the rationale to consider a role in the field of artificial intelligence and provided a high-level overview of the variety of roles within the AI industry.

Notes

1   Spataro, S (2020) 2 years of digital transformation in 2 months, www.microsoft. com/en-us/microsoft-365/blog/2020/04/30/2-years-digital-transformation-2-months/ (archived at https://perma.cc/HZB2-HCW8)
2   Data science, en.wikipedia.org/wiki/Data_science
3   Automated machine learning, en.wikipedia.org/wiki/Automated_machine_learning (archived at https://perma.cc/7MP3-6HBF)

CHAPTER TWO

AI myths

There are many common AI myths that need to be addressed to ensure you have a solid foundation of understanding about AI and don't become part of the hype machine that has been building steam over the past few years.

It can be easy to fall into the trap, to believe the noise and to take a dystopian perspective of how AI might advance in the coming years. Some are concerned that AI will either intentionally or mistakenly destroy humanity, to remove us as the major source of destruction on planet Earth. Others seem to think we might become slaves to the AI overlords, with the rise of machines becoming more intelligent, stronger and fitter (from a Darwinian perspective). Or we might become as important to AI as ants are to us, seen not even as pets but just as an annoyance that co-exists but isn't really needed.

I have a more positive (even utopian) perspective of how AI will evolve and support us. After all, AI is just another technology tool we are building to help us, and worst case we can simply turn it off, or run it in a simulation. I don't see a scenario where we would remove the human in the loop and fully automate everything to the extent that we risk our own existence – this simply would not happen.

There are several reasons why myths and misunderstandings persist when it comes to the subject of artificial intelligence. Here are some key rationales:

1 **Hollywood portrayals:** Movies and popular culture often depict AI in exaggerated and fantastical ways, leading to misconceptions. Films like *The Terminator* and *The Matrix* showcase AI as superintelligent, malevolent entities, which is far from the current state or foreseeable future of AI technology.

2 **Lack of understanding:** AI is a complex field that encompasses various subfields like machine learning, neural networks and natural language processing. Many people lack the technical knowledge to fully comprehend these concepts, leading to simplified and inaccurate beliefs.

3 **Media hype:** Media often sensationalizes AI breakthroughs and research, presenting them as more advanced and capable than they actually are. This creates unrealistic expectations and fuels myths about AI's current capabilities.

4 **Anthropomorphism:** People tend to anthropomorphize AI, attributing human-like qualities and intentions to machines. This can lead to misconceptions that AI possesses consciousness, emotions or malicious intent.

5 **Fear of the unknown:** Fear and uncertainty about the future of AI can lead to myths and misconceptions. People may overestimate the risks and capabilities of AI due to the unknown nature of its development.

6 **Marketing hype:** Companies and organizations often use AI as a buzzword to promote their products and services, sometimes stretching the definition of AI. This can create confusion about what AI actually is and what it can do.

7 **Ethical concerns:** Discussions about AI ethics, bias and the potential for job displacement can amplify fears and misconceptions about AI. While these are legitimate concerns, they can be taken to extremes that do not reflect the nuanced reality of AI technology.

8 **Rapid advancements:** AI is a rapidly evolving field, and what was true a few years ago may no longer be accurate. This dynamic nature of AI can lead to outdated beliefs and inflated expectations of future advancements.

9 **Lack of transparency:** Some AI systems operate as 'black boxes', meaning their decision-making processes are not easily explainable. This lack of transparency can contribute to myths and suspicions about AI's inner workings.

In summary, AI myths persist due to a combination of factors, driven primarily by portrayals in popular culture, media sensationalism and a lack of technical understanding. Let's dive into some of the most widely shared AI myths.

Below we take some of the most common or widely promoted AI myths and look to provide a different opinion to counter the argument.

Myth 1: AI is just a fad that will soon fade away

One of the most common misconceptions about AI is that it's just a passing fad. However, nothing could be further from the truth. The reality is that AI has been around for decades, but it has only recently begun to enter mainstream consciousness due largely to advances in computing power and data storage capacity, combined with the utility of the latest models (including LLMs) that can deliver many different use-cases.

These days, businesses of all sizes are beginning to realize the potential of AI and are starting to invest in this transformative technology. In fact, according to a recent report from International Data Corporation (IDC), worldwide spending on AI-centric systems will pass $300 billion by 2026.[1]

It is difficult to see how AI will fade away, as the benefits it provides are so far-ranging and impactful that once implemented it is unlikely that firms will decide to switch off.

However, we have seen the enthusiasm for AI wane before, with what is referred to as AI winters.[2] This is when the mainstream expectation of AI is much greater than what is technically possible at the time, the investors and businesses get disillusioned and the hype focus moves onto something else in the short term. But history has shown us that in time, with the next step-change innovation such as a new learning algorithm or approach, the world comes back to AI as the most interesting and advanced technology looks to move us closer to the moonshot of artificial general intelligence or superintelligence.

Myth 2: Only big businesses can afford AI

Another common misconception about AI is that it's only accessible to big businesses with deep pockets. However, this simply isn't true. Thanks to cloud-based services like Amazon Web Services (AWS) and Google Cloud Platform (GCP), even small businesses can now take advantage of AI without breaking the bank.

For example, AWS offers a wide range of services for building and deploying AI applications, including pre-trained models that can be used for tasks like image recognition and text classification. GCP also offers several ready-to-use machine learning models that can be deployed with just a few clicks. Other cloud platforms also provide a wide range of AI capabilities, including Microsoft Azure (which has now integrated the capabilities from OpenAI), IBM Cloud, Oracle Cloud and Alibaba.

Certainly, the big organizations have had the funding and budgets to invest in AI innovations over the last five years or so, to explore how the technology might apply to their business operations and in many cases adopt early implementations to provide productivity efficiencies, such as customer chatbots. However, we are now seeing more and more SME businesses, with limited budgets and resources, also exploring how AI can help improve business operations and productivity.

The challenge for these businesses is that while implementing the relatively easy use-cases can be done without major investment, for some of the more challenging problems it will be likely that a custom solution is needed, which will require some level of investment to deliver. Only by understanding that and prioritizing the AI use-cases, so that only the ones that can return on the investment and deliver a solution to a specific business problem, will any AI programme be seen as successful. The key for smaller businesses with limited resources is to be selective and focus on solving real problems.

Myth 3: Machines will soon replace humans in the workforce

This myth likely stems from Hollywood movies like *The Terminator* and *The Matrix*, which paint a dystopian future in which machines have taken over the world and humans are nothing more than slaves (or worse). Out of all the myths we list, this one is the most controversial and, in some ways, closest to realization.

In reality, however, there's no need to worry about an impending robot uprising. Machines are not going to replace all humans in the workforce any time soon – and they're not designed to. Instead, machines will complement human workers by taking on repetitive and dangerous tasks so that humans can focus on more creative work.

We will see continued human-in-the-loop processes where AI will augment our human decision making by analysing the huge quantities of data that is difficult for us to make sense of. For the majority, our jobs will change, improve, with automation and AI capabilities supporting our daily tasks.

However, there will be some jobs and roles that very soon can be fully automated with technology. Like any disruptive technology, the working environment is going to change, and we will all need to adapt. Some roles will disappear, others will be created, and most will be augmented with technology. The challenge for some is how hard it is to quickly reskill and find a new role that suits your skills and experience. Depending on the speed of change, this will become a significant problem for countries, and governments will need to work with businesses and industries to find appropriate solutions to protect and support those workers who will be displaced.

How this industrial revolution differs from previous ones is that AI touches every industry and every role, so the potential disruption is significant if it is not properly managed, controlled and limited. How governments and regulators oversee and guide this change will be decisive in how well we all can adapt to a world with intelligent technology by our side.

Myth 4: AI is too difficult to implement

While it may seem that getting started and implementing the first use of AI within your company is too difficult, there is a huge amount of information and support available to allow you to have a successful first implementation. One of the ways to improve your chances of success is to select a use-case that is internal to the firm (limiting exposure to your clients) and is lower in complexity compared to other potential use-case candidates.

There are so many tools and applications available now that getting started with AI is easier than it has ever been, allowing companies of all sizes to experiment with the use of AI across many different areas. Certainly, getting started simply and learning by doing is a key approach that will allow people within the organization to learn gradually and explore different ways AI can add value to the business. Scaling AI across an organization can be more difficult and there will be some roadblocks and challenges that need to be navigated.

There are many ways you can improve your chances of success with AI adoption, from understanding the vision and mission of AI for the future success of your firm, to guiding the approach of implementation from first innovative proofs of concept to scaled rollout of AI across the company. There are also many information resources available that can support the process of understanding AI abilities and how to properly implement. Another key to success is defining your company's AI strategy, as this will help you determine what is needed to lay the foundations for deploying AI at scale.

There are challenges to AI implementation; some of this is due to the lack of standardization for both the technology and the process. However, there are advisors and experienced data scientists who can help you and your firm define best practices to ensure successful deployments.

Myth 5: AI will never be able to replicate human levels of Intelligence

Some industry practitioners believe that true advanced intelligence capabilities simply cannot be replicated using silicon-based technologies. There is no evidence to either support or deny this proposition. Certainly, at this stage, there is nothing concrete that makes this a real concern. However, we do have a lot more to investigate and many specific intelligent capabilities to build, so only time will tell. Personally, I do not think there is anything within biological minds that cannot be functionally duplicated with other technologies.

AI is a multidisciplinary subject and will likely need contributions from many areas to move us towards human levels of intelligence. It will also require a wide range of methodologies and techniques to deliver anything close to the highly complex abilities that we see with human intelligence. Many believe with the recent advances in generative AI that we are much closer to artificial general intelligence; however, expert opinion on when AGI will be achieved is hugely divided – anywhere from 10 years to 1,000 years.

What is clear is the desire of the AI industry to work towards and achieve this moonshot, as it will create significant competitor advantage for the person or company that first delivers an AGI-capable system.

The industry is focused on machine learning at the moment, but it will need to take a broader perspective on all the core capabilities of intelligence if it is to replicate human levels of intelligence.

Myth 6: You need to be a technologist to work in the field of AI

While technical skills are valuable and essential for certain roles in AI development, the field of AI is diverse and offers opportunities for individuals with a wide range of backgrounds and expertise.

In essence, the field of AI is multidisciplinary, and it welcomes individuals with diverse skills and backgrounds. While technical expertise can be advantageous in certain roles, there is a growing demand for professionals who can contribute to AI from non-technical angles, whether it be in ethics, strategy, communication or other areas. So, you don't necessarily need to be a technologist to have a meaningful and impactful career in AI.

Some of the potential areas and roles that do not require detailed technical knowledge or background include:

1 **AI ethics and policy:** As AI technologies become more widespread, there is a growing need for experts in AI ethics and policy. Professionals in this field work on the ethical, legal and societal implications of AI, ensuring that AI systems are developed and used responsibly.

2 **AI strategy and management:** Companies and organizations need individuals who can formulate AI strategies, make informed decisions about AI adoption and manage AI projects. Business acumen and strategic thinking are highly valuable in these roles.

3 **AI research and analysis:** AI generates vast amounts of data, and there is a need for analysts and researchers who can interpret this data, draw insights and inform decision making. Strong analytical skills are essential in this area.

4 **User experience (UX) and design:** Designers and UX experts play a critical role in creating user-friendly AI interfaces and applications. They ensure that AI technologies are accessible and intuitive for users.

5 **AI education and training:** Educators and trainers are needed to teach AI concepts to a broad audience, from students to professionals. Developing educational materials and courses on AI can be a valuable contribution.

6 **AI journalism and communication:** Journalists and communicators who can explain AI developments, breakthroughs and their societal impacts to the general public help bridge the gap between technologists and the wider community.

7 **AI sales and marketing:** Companies selling AI products and services require sales and marketing professionals who can communicate the value of AI solutions to potential customers and clients.

8 **AI project management:** Managing AI projects involves coordinating various aspects, from technical development to team collaboration. Project management skills are vital in ensuring AI projects are executed successfully.

9 **AI legal and intellectual property:** Lawyers specializing in AI law can help navigate the legal complexities surrounding AI, including intellectual property, privacy and liability issues.

Myth 7: Building AI will become fully automated

AI itself is being used to automate various tasks and processes, but the process of creating and developing AI systems is far from becoming fully automated.

While AI can automate many tasks and improve efficiency, the process of building AI systems remains a collaborative effort that relies on human expertise, creativity and oversight at various stages. AI development is not fully automated and is unlikely to become so in the foreseeable future, as it involves complex decision making, domain-specific knowledge and ethical considerations that require human involvement.

Here's why:

1 **Complexity of AI development:** Developing AI systems is a complex, multidisciplinary process that involves various stages, including problem formulation, data collection and preprocessing, algorithm selection and training, model evaluation, and deployment. Each of these stages requires human expertise and judgment.

2 **Problem understanding:** AI systems are designed to solve specific problems or perform tasks. Defining the problem, understanding the nuances and setting the objectives often requires human domain expertise. An AI system cannot automatically discern the objectives without clear human guidance.

3 **Data quality and preprocessing:** AI models rely heavily on data, and ensuring the quality, relevance and fairness of the data used for training is a crucial step. Data preprocessing, cleaning and labelling often require human intervention to handle ambiguous or complex data.

4 **Algorithm selection and tuning:** Choosing the right algorithms and models for a given task is a critical decision in AI development. It requires human expertise to evaluate the suitability of different techniques and to fine-tune them for optimal performance.

5 **Model interpretability and ethical considerations:** Understanding how AI models make decisions and ensuring they are ethically designed are important considerations. Human oversight is required to interpret model outputs, identify biases and make ethical decisions about model behaviour.

6 **Continuous monitoring and maintenance:** AI systems require ongoing monitoring and maintenance to adapt to changing conditions and ensure they perform as intended. This involves human oversight to detect issues, update models and make necessary improvements.

7 **Creativity and innovation:** Many breakthroughs in AI research are the result of creative thinking and innovation. Human researchers and engineers continually push the boundaries of what AI can do, coming up with new algorithms and approaches.

8 **Regulatory and compliance requirements:** Compliance with legal and regulatory frameworks, such as data protection laws and industry standards, often necessitates human expertise to navigate complex requirements and ensure AI systems are compliant.

9 **User interaction and experience:** Designing user-friendly interfaces for AI applications and considering user needs and feedback require human-centred design principles, which cannot be fully automated.

10 **Contextual understanding:** AI systems lack a deep understanding of context and common-sense reasoning, which humans possess. Human judgment is crucial for interpreting and acting upon AI-generated information.

Myth 8: AI is infallible and always right

AI systems, like any technology, are not infallible, and they can make mistakes or provide incorrect results for several reasons.

It's important to remember that AI is a tool created by humans, and its performance depends on the quality of data, the design of the model and the expertise of the developers. While AI can be incredibly powerful and accurate in many cases, it is not a guarantee of perfection, and its limitations and potential for errors should be taken into consideration when using AI systems. Human supervision and critical thinking remain essential when making decisions based on AI-generated insights.

Some of the issues making AI error-prone include:

1 **Data bias:** AI systems learn from historical data, and if the training data is biased or incomplete, the AI can perpetuate those biases. This can result in unfair or biased decisions, particularly in applications like hiring, lending or criminal justice.

2 **Inadequate training data:** If the training dataset is not representative or lacks diversity, AI models may not generalize well to new or unseen situations. They might perform poorly when faced with data that differs from their training data.

3 **Model limitations:** AI models have limitations based on their architecture and the algorithms they use. They may not be well suited for certain tasks or may struggle with complex reasoning and context understanding.

4 **Noisy data:** Noise or errors in data can negatively affect AI performance. Even small amounts of incorrect data can lead to inaccurate results.

5 **Changing environments:** AI models are trained on historical data, and they may not adapt well to rapidly changing environments or unforeseen events. They lack real-time learning abilities.

6 **Adversarial attacks:** AI systems can be vulnerable to attacks that are specifically designed to exploit their weaknesses. For example, adding imperceptible noise to an image can trick image recognition systems.

7 **Uncertainty:** AI models often provide confidence scores or probabilities with their predictions. High uncertainty can indicate that the model is unsure about a particular prediction, and it may not always be correct.

8 **Ethical and moral dilemmas:** AI may make decisions based on data and algorithms, but it cannot make ethical or moral judgments. Decisions made by AI systems may not align with human values and ethics.

9 **Technical errors:** Like any software, AI systems can have technical bugs or issues that affect their performance and reliability.

10 **Human oversight:** In many AI applications, human oversight is essential to validate AI-generated results and correct errors. Relying solely on AI without human review can lead to incorrect outcomes.

Other myths

There are many other AI-related myths, and new ones are surfacing all the time as the field of study develops and the capabilities delivered advance:

1 **Human skills are irrelevant:** The belief that only technical skills matter when working with AI, neglecting the importance of human skills like creativity, empathy and critical thinking.

2 **AI solves all business problems:** The idea that AI is a one-size-fits-all solution that can address any business challenge, without considering the need for careful problem framing and context-specific solutions.

3 **AI-driven innovation:** The myth that AI can drive innovation on its own, without the need for human ideation, creativity, and strategic thinking.

4 **Permanent AI implementation:** The misconception that AI systems can be deployed once and require no further adjustments or maintenance, disregarding the need for continuous monitoring and adaptation. This is a key element of AI and machine learning systems at the moment, and is needed because the underlying data changes over time.

Future AI myths

We will look at the future perspective for AI in a later chapter but let's touch on how different perspectives can feed into the myths and misunderstandings of AI. With technology commentary, one can take either a utopian or dystopian perspective, seeing the balance in utility being either a force for good or evil.

There is significant concern around the ethics, governance and control of advanced AI, leading towards artificial general intelligence and superintelligence. How we avoid the technology spinning out of control or potentially creating an extinction event that wipes out all of humanity is a significant concern, as we may not get a second chance to get this right.

The fact is, we are creating an artificial intelligence which might one day rival or even surpass our own collective human intelligence, superseding us as the dominant species on planet Earth.

This rapidly changing technology advancement is such that it naturally creates an environment for myths and misunderstanding, in some cases amplified by those who can gain financial and commercial benefit from this hype and sensational headlines.

Dystopia

Some people worry that AI will ultimately become so smart that it will find a way to control the world. While this makes great material for Hollywood movies, in all probability it is unlikely to happen. AI, like any technology, is a tool, a tool that we control and are able to switch off if required. However, regardless of how unlikely this might be, it is a possibility, But we build failsafes and tollgates into programming to prevent the mere possibility of any fully automated takeover by AI agents.

Utopia

While this also has the makings of a Hollywood blockbuster, it has a more welcomed outcome for humans: living in a land with no suffering, no poverty, no illness and no crime. The utopian view is one where AI helps us solve all the most difficult problems we currently have, including climate change and the energy crisis. This seems achievable but sometimes also too good to be true. There has to be a catch, a downside, a trade-off that we will need to make for all this benefit. Maybe it will be our gradual distancing from the technology we built to solve these problems, a distance over time, that means we eventually forget how to build and maintain such systems.

Neutropia

With dystopian and utopian perspectives being the two extremes, a neutropian view takes a path between the two, taking elements of both and pursuing developments within the realm of reality.

We should recognize that we will likely find ourselves in a world with a fusion of AI technology and humanity, with both positives and negatives in play. With this outlook, we approach AI with the most rational and level-headed perspective.

Myth busting

The field of AI is highly specialized, with the majority of the population having only a partial understanding of how the technology works. In addition, the field is advancing at such a tremendous rate that it is difficult for most people to differentiate between what is science fiction and what is science fact.

Sir Arthur C Clarke's third law states that 'Any sufficiently advanced technology is indistinguishable from magic'.[3] This is what we are starting to see with the advances of AI.

Obviously with such an impactful and important technology, it is sensible to take a cautionary approach, highlighting the full range of considerations, raising awareness and ensuring that we put the right level of pressure on those who are shaping the future with AI to make sure they do so in a responsible and trustworthy manner.

But also, those who do work in the industry have an obligation to dispel these myths and help people to truly understand the beauty and the challenges of AI-powered technology.

AI myths are often born more out of a misunderstanding of the technology than a deep-rooted fear. We will continue to be amazed by the abilities and what is possible with AI, but it means we just need to invest in gaining an understanding to help us alleviate our worries and concerns. However, with any disruptive new technology we will see issues, failures and some unintended consequences that will need to be managed and controlled to limit the impact and avoid scaremongering and fear that could set back AI innovation for decades.

Notes

1 Shirer, M (2022) Worldwide spending on AI-centric systems will pass $300 billion by 2026, according to IDC, https://www.idc.com/getdoc. jsp?containerId=prUS49670322# (archived at https://perma.cc/W2JN-FLL8)

2 AI winter, https://en.wikipedia.org/wiki/AI_winter (archived at https://perma. cc/8PTA-Y6MP)

3 Clarke's three laws, https://en.wikipedia.org/wiki/Clarke%27s_three_laws (archived at https://perma.cc/K3WC-B94F)

CHAPTER THREE

Applications of AI

While AI research is looking to advance the fundamentals of artificial intelligence, applied AI is the area that looks to use AI to solve real-world problems and provide actionable insights and predictive forecasting to help with both strategic and tactical decision making.

Both the applied and research areas of AI have significant potential and opportunities for your career in AI. The beauty of applied AI is that you also need knowledge of the relevant industry sector. It may be that you already have industry experience and expertise, or you want to use the transition into AI to learn a new business area.

While various industries are adopting AI at differing rates, the reality is that most, if not all industries are now actively onboarding AI in some part of their business and will likely expand this adoption over the coming years. If not, competitors in the same industry will do so and gain significant benefits that will make them a stronger challenge in the future. Businesses need to innovate to survive, and currently that innovation is the utilization of

FIGURE 3.1   The 10 stages of AI adoption

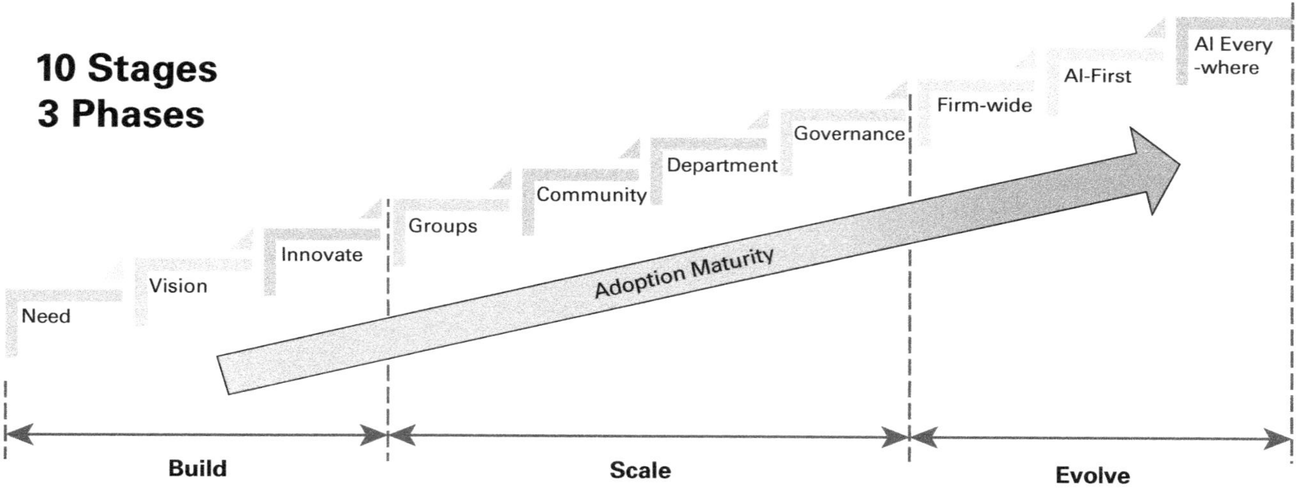

10 Stages
3 Phases

Need

Vision

Innovate

Groups

Community

Department

Governance

Firm-wide

AI-First

AI Every-where

Adoption Maturity

Build

Scale

Evolve

AI-powered technologies. The competitor advantage from early adoption of AI can be dramatically impactful to businesses, from productivity improvements to enhancements to products and services.

In this chapter we will showcase several industries that are at various stages of AI utilization, highlighting some of the main application areas and benefits. Typically, an organization goes through 10 stages of AI adoption, or, more simply put, as three phases of AI enablement (shown in Figure 3.1). Firms will move from one stage to another at different rates, having to overcome various challenges along the way, a common journey for any digital transformation programme.

We provide insights into a range of industries; some have been at the cutting edge of AI adoption for a while, and others are only just starting to explore the benefits of using AI. Leveraging AI has, until recently, been something of a luxury, only available to the largest of firms with knowledgeable people with access to computational resources and quantities of data that are not easily accessible to smaller companies. But now organizations of all sizes can access the necessary components to create AI predictive models and integrate them with existing applications.

Healthcare

AI within medical and healthcare applications has only been explored as a research activity but is rarely involved in mainstream applications. However, the Covid-19 pandemic changed the acceptance of AI technologies across many different applications, from drug repurposing to resource allocation, prediction of the spread of the disease, and even robots cleaning hospitals.

During the pandemic, we also saw a dramatic increase in well-being applications leveraging AI capabilities to support the needs of individuals at risk to due increased insolation caused by social distancing, quarantines and separation from loved ones.

The longer-term ambitions of AI in the medical sector include more precision medicines aligned to individuals' DNA and specific needs, together with helping to cure and even prevent many of the illnesses and diseases we are currently victim to.

Finance

The financial services sector has been one of the first to adopt the use of AI. There are so many potential applications across the industry. Specific to the industry include algorithmic trading, trading recommendations, fraud detection and risk management, and more generally customer service, process automation, data reconciliations, report generation, system monitoring and predictive maintenance.

With high volumes of transactions and many repeatable tasks needing to be performed daily, the scope for intelligent automation across front-, middle- and back-office areas is massive. Using technology to help cope with fluctuations in daily volumes takes the pressure off manual processing and allows the human resources to deal with the more difficult data breaks and customer queries.

Customers are now expecting a more personalized service with more specific recommendations tailored to the individual's needs and set of circumstances – which means better data analytics and insights capabilities to provide these individually targeted suggestions.

It is not just the big investment banks that have implemented AI; it's retail banks, investment and hedge funds, fintech start-ups and challenger banks as well as the insurance sector. AI regulations are a key aspect of financial services, with the need for decision transparency and explainability major considerations.

CASE STUDY   Nuon.AI

The team behind Nuon.AI have extensive experience within the insurance industry and have built a real-time pricing platform using cutting-edge AI technologies including reinforcement learning to create a product suite that can deliver exceptional results for their clients. They provide their platform to insurance companies, brokers and managing general agents, working across a range of sectors including motor, travel and home insurance.

The technology they have developed has helped, for example, to drive up sales by 31 per cent for a UK motor insurer that is competing with the bigger insurance companies. Not only did sales increase but they managed to also increase premiums by 28 per cent, with only an aggregate cost of 1.7 per cent discounting. The proprietary AI algorithms created by Nuon took the strain out of finding optimal price points to compete more effectively and efficiently, while significantly growing both sales and premiums without the need for heavy discounting.

Essentially, the AI platform acts like a radar, solving a fundamental problem for insurers and brokers: how to gain insights into changing market conditions fast enough to compete profitably.

Sales and marketing

Generally, for any type of business, the activities of sales and marketing could have been supported by basic AI capabilities for some time. However, generative AI has opened many more opportunities for AI to enhance productivity in this area.

Sales chatbots (and customer support chatbots) have been in existence for several years, although the range of conversations has been limited to well-defined dialogue flows. Not so with conversational and generative AI – it opens a much wider ability to engage in more detail with existing and potential customers.

Marketing can now benefit greatly from the capabilities of generative AI, helping to fast-track the creation of articles and blog posts to support any marketing campaign or sales promotion.

The technology now allows for much greater personalization, enabling more precise and targeted sales activities and helping to improve conversion rates. This can be applied to upsell and cross-sell promotions too, all looking to improve the revenue opportunities of the business with better, more appropriate and targeted communications to prospects and existing customers.

Linking AI tools into the workflow of sales and marketing processes will be key to improved productivity and personalization for the marketing promotions and sales activities of any business.

Education

The goal of AI within education is to help improve and accelerate the learning of students, helping to better target the areas of support needed by creating more personalized learning syllabuses that adapt to ongoing assessments and educational analytics.

AI in the classroom can determine specific needs and help teachers to deliver the most targeted support to ensure no child is left behind and we all get the best start in life.

There is a significant challenge with students using AI tools such as ChatGPT to help them complete assignments. Different institutions have varying opinions on this approach, and it is making the role of teachers more difficult, especially when it comes to assessing the pupils' skills and knowledge.

Universities and schools will need to adapt to these new tools that students can leverage and look to prepare them for their technology-enhanced working life which will be augmented with many intelligence applications and systems, working side-by-side with the human workforce.

Industry and manufacturing

The manufacturing sector has been a little slower to adopt AI technologies, with a few exceptions. One of the first most obvious applications in this area is that of predictive mainte-nance, helping to predict, before it happens, when a piece of machinery needs to be serviced or a part fixed to avoid any cata-strophic failures or unscheduled downtime.

The aircraft industry is a wonderful case study for this, as we know the engine manufacturer Rolls Royce has many sensors on each engine, monitoring its performance in real time. All this real-time data is sent back to their headquarters for detailed anal-ysis, with any anomaly flagged as an indicator for investigation.

We also see digital twins being used to help model and simu-late manufacturing processes, or even buildings (such as hospitals), to allow what-if style scenarios to be simulated, help-ing with the planning of contingencies if required based on any particular future situations. This can also help with supply chain and other detailed processes and procedures.

Agriculture and environmental monitoring

Opportunities for AI to support this sector span the entire value chain, from farming and picking to transport, processing, ship-ping and manufacture. Intelligent automation and AI analytics can play a significant role in every part of the food production process.

From the monitoring of crop health to helping to improve the yield and quality of output, predictive analytics can provide valuable insights and alert people to potential issues ahead of time.

We even see AI being used in food development, aligning to customer preferences and trends for flavours, textures, aromas and nutritional aspects.

In addition to these core value chain opportunities, data analytics and machine learning can be used to explore customer insights, from social listening and sentiment analysis to customer engagement via chatbots and sales forecasting.

Entertainment and creative industries

It is clear that generative AI is going to significantly disrupt the entertainment and creativity industry. It already has started. From text generation to image and video, the capability of generative AI is improving at pace. Only today, as I write this, did I see an announcement for a news channel that will be completely AI-generated in terms of the presenter and studio – it will be presenting real-world news, but potentially the perspective of the reporting will be customized to the preferences of the individual viewer.

It is likely that we will see much more hyper-personalized media, generated on the fly for each individual consumer in a way and perspective they want.

We will also see fully AI-generated TV programmes and films soon, and potentially one day these can be generated in real-time, allowing us to truly interact and determine the plot and story direction.

This is going to be a significant disruption to the current media industry, and it will be very interesting to see how it embraces this new technological revolution in the next few years.

Energy and utilities

There are three aspects to this sector: the first is focused on the industry itself, the second on the consumer, and the third is future-looking towards green and clean energy tech.

For the industry itself, potential use-cases include predictive maintenance, grid management, consumption optimization in buildings, energy trading and risk management, battery storage optimization, as well as safety and efficiency.

For the consumer, smart meters are just the start, as leveraging data analytics to help better predict consumption trends and come up with strategies and changes to activities that can help save energy without major impacts on lifestyle will become more common in the future.

AI can have a massive impact on the field of green and clean energy, from designing new products to delivering more energy-efficient buildings (with the combination of IoT and smart buildings), carbon footprint analysis and reduction, and renewable energy forecasting.

Government and public services

While governments and public services tend to be more conservative with the adoption of new technologies, taking a more risk-averse stance, the benefit of leveraging AI is as clear to see for them as it is for any other commercial business.

Ultimately, it is about providing a range of services and products to their community of users with a limited number of available resources to do so. Productivity gains can prove invaluable to deliver better-targeted services to a high number of deserving cases.

Efficiency and effectiveness will play a major role in the adoption of AI-related capabilities over the coming years in this sector.

From a national perspective, it is not just about how a government might use AI to deliver services better. They also need to look at the broader impacts and consequences of the widespread use of the technology across the nation and how this affects its citizens. What regulation might be needed, and safeguards and concerns around data privacy and individuals' rights, need to be considered.

Many governments are looking at these potential issues seriously, with the EU AI Act,[1] the US executive order on the use of AI[2] and the UK hosting the world's first AI Safety Summit.[3]

Legal and compliance

The legal sector has been exploring the capabilities of AI, in particular natural language processing to help with the volume of documents they typically need to review. Comparing similar contractual documents and highlighting the differences is a time-consuming, repetitive and mundane task.

The sector is moving into more advanced applications, including digital legal advisors, analysis of case materials, forming legal arguments and providing information as part of the evidence in criminal cases.

However, there have been problems with the use of such technologies, aligned to the fundamental issue of generative AI having the potential to hallucinate facts and even laws as part of its output. Therefore, caution is needed in any highly regulated industry with these new technologies to ensure they are working accurately and as expected.

While the industry has these challenges to overcome, the technology will surely be impactful, changing the ways legal firms work, and the services delivered to both businesses and individuals.

Supply chain and logistics

Much of supply chain and logistics can be automated and optimized with the application of data insights, analytics and predictive modelling, from product demand estimation to optimizing delivery routes. While this may not be the most exciting of application areas, the impact of AI tooling in this space can and will have a significant impact on our environment and the cost of delivering our parcels to our homes.

A combination of AI, automation and robotics will create a dramatic change to the end-to-end processes of supply chains, with the challenges around the last mile and 100 yards to the doorstep becoming more automated and therefore easier to deal with.

In the future, we might well have a delivery assistant android or drone that supports that last part for supply chain logistics.

Human resources and talent management

As with any function within the operations of business, HR and talent management is no different, with a range of potential applications for AI. This includes talent acquisition, candidate screening, interview insights and workforce analytics, as well as analysis of employee engagement and performance evaluation.

CASE STUDY WeSoar.AI

Utilizing AI to augment and support the workforce is an area that most organizations will be focused on as the use of AI tools becomes more commonplace. Increasing the productivity of the enterprise by supporting and improving the performance of the human workforce is key to the future of companies as they embrace their AI-powered future, together with an approach that uses the power of positive psychology, specifically appreciative inquiry, which revolves around strengths, opportunities, aspirations and results.

The WeSoar platform uses a range of data analytics and AI technologies to deliver optimized team performance, improving engagement and motivating employees to achieve peak performance with light-touch interactions within a mobile app.

The team at WeSoar also rapidly embraced the capabilities of generative and conversational AI, leveraging the concept of a digital assistant to deliver many of the functional aspects of the platform. This is combined with AI-based nudges and reminders to deliver more action-based outcomes.

Non-profit and social impact

The application of AI within the charity, non-profit and social impact sectors is increasingly important; the potential benefits across everything from supply chain to improving donations are tremendous. For disaster response, healthcare access and education initiatives, AI can have a positive impact on the delivery and efficiency of these services.

There are so many amazing applications that are helping individuals deal with and overcome disabilities, combat human trafficking, enhance fundraising and donor engagement, and improve social welfare and service matching.

The potential benefits that AI can deliver in this application area are significant and truly align with the AI for Good ethos that many practitioners in the field share.

Charities are often resource-constrained and would welcome additional help and support to leverage the benefits of AI-based insights. DataKind is an organization I have worked with previously that helps match data science skills with organizations looking for help with projects.

It is so important that we understand the impact and ethical considerations of AI technologies, ensuring that responsible AI practices are followed in the non-profit sector.

Emerging and cross-industry applications

There are many industries that cut across the field of AI, enabling it – for example, quantum computing, which has the potential to dramatically accelerate the advancement of AI. Computer hardware is another example, with the likes of NVIDIA, ARM, Graphcore and others producing dedicated processors for AI acceleration (specifically neural networks).

Deep tech

Deep tech covers a range of industries (and technologies) but ultimately is looking to build commercial applications that are made possible through the latest scientific research. Many deep tech companies spend years in R&D creating new products on the back of advanced technology breakthroughs. Some leverage AI as part of their research efforts, potentially combined with other scientific discoveries. These types of companies offer some of the most challenging opportunities but also the most rewarding (at least from a purely scientific basis).

CASE STUDY Warwick University Deep Tech Innovation Centre

Many universities are increasingly helping students, alumni and staff to explore ways to commercialize their research innovations. Warwick University in the UK has a whole innovation district focused on supporting scientific entrepreneurs. The innovation district has several centres, each running different programmes for various industries or areas of focus. The programmes help founders to create products from their inventions, build teams and seek funding for their businesses to grow. This also helps to educate and inform those interested in start-ups as a career option. The Deep Tech programme is a six-month series of training workshops and learning sessions, business and technical mentoring, and match-making with potential team members, culminating with a *Dragons' Den*-style pitch event.

Final thoughts

While previous industrial revolutions gravitated around one key industry, the disruptive nature of AI is that it can be applied to many, if not all, industries. It also impacts all departments and functions within a business, making the potential of AI to change the commercial landscape and the economics of business models significant. We have yet to see the full impact of this, and the resulting aftershocks will create both new opportunities and challenges we will all need to navigate. Some industries and companies will prosper, others will fall victim to this new order of intelligent automation.

But those with a desire to work in the field of AI will find boundless opportunities in any number of application areas and industries. The question will be more about what area and industry you want to specialize in.

The future of applied AI will be to deliver more capable analytics and insights that support the core functions and mission of the business, connecting intelligent decision making across the organization, delivering a more customized and personalized service to customers and helping the business to anticipate the future and plan ahead to minimize issues.

The functionality of AI means that businesses need to raise the bar and deliver more value to customers than ever before, through personalization, efficiencies, quality improvement or new products and services. The rate of innovation and changes that companies will need to deliver will put additional pressures on the management teams and will require firms to look for advantage wherever they can find it.

With this widespread adoption and the race to benefit from AI-powered applications and functions, the opportunities for careers in AI will only increase over the coming years – those who can apply AI to solve challenging problems will be in high demand.

Notes

1   EU AI Act: first regulation on artificial intelligence, www.europarl.europa.eu/
news/en/headlines/society/20230601STO93804/eu-ai-act-first-regulation-on-
artificial-intelligence (archived at https://perma.cc/A9L7-8JG3)

2   Executive Order on the Safe, Secure, and Trustworthy Development and Use of Artificial Intelligence, www.whitehouse.gov/briefing-room/presidential-actions/2023/10/30/executive-order-on-the-safe-secure-and-trustworthy-development-and-use-of-artificial-intelligence/ (archived at https://perma.cc/L2VF-9QQN)

3   AI Safety Summit 2023, www.gov.uk/government/topical-events/ai-safety-summit-2023 (archived at https://perma.cc/K2SS-BD2S)

CHAPTER FOUR

A future perspective

So far the AI journey has been a real rollercoaster, with two previous AI winters (where the enthusiasm and funding for AI cooled off for a period of time). While interest in AI has been slowly increasing over the last decade or so, it was not widely accepted or utilized until recently; 2023 was a breakthrough year, showcasing AI as a general-purpose tool that was becoming a truly mass-market technology for the first time in its history.

This momentum has since accelerated, with significant developments (and investments) from all the key players in the tech industry to maximize the opportunity, as CEOs and CTOs of firms large and small seek the potential benefits of productivity gains and functional enhancements from integrating the latest AI capabilities.

The AI landscape and environment are very dynamic, with changes happening at a blistering rate, making it challenging for even the most informed practitioners to keep up with the new developments in the field that are being released on a daily basis.

While the technology is evolving rapidly, governments and regulators are doing their best to keep up too, but they are having to balance the benefits of innovation dominance and economic prosperity with the ethical and safety concerns and consequences of allowing the technology firms too much freedom. This is a fine balance, and governments have differing opinions on what is the right level of oversight and control. Simplistically, the United States favours big tech, Europe is more on the side of the consumer, while the UK is trying to find a balance to allow AI innovation but with the safe controls of responsible AI governance.

There is likely to be significant innovation in the coming years around AI ethics and trustworthiness, data privacy and trust, audit, governance and control. The UK government hosted the world's first global AI Safety Summit in 2023 to get global agreement on some of these major concerns, signing the Bletchley Park Agreement[1] and agreeing to set up two global AI institutions to test frontier models.

However, we must appreciate that the AI industry is only 70 years old, and while this might seem a long time to many, most of the significant progress has only happened in the last two decades, and our learning algorithms, paradigms and architectures are still very simplistic compared to the diversity of neural patterns we see in the human brain. While not conclusive, this does seem to suggest we have a long way to go before we can achieve deep levels of intelligent behaviours and abilities comparable to our own human intelligence. Some will argue that the advances we have seen in recent months with large language models, conversational and generative AI are testament to the significant progress we have made, and that the moonshot of AGI is much closer than previously thought. However, there are many other AI experts who challenge the true capabilities of these LLMs and highlight a need for more a robust and complete solution.

The energy consumption of these massive models is also a concern, especially when you consider the energy utilization of the human brain (at about 20 per cent of the body's total energy consumption, that's approximately 0.3 kilowatt hours per day[2]), while an LLM can take up to an estimated 10 gigawatt hour to train (roughly equivalent to the yearly electricity consumption of over 1,000 US households[3]) and in many cases still require a GPU to run the model in inference mode. IBM have a grand challenge to produce AI that has similar energy utilization to that of a human mind, which is an admirable objective. The potential of commercial-scale quantum computing may also help to reduce training time and to some degree energy consumption too.

Ultimately, there is likely to be decades more research and development needed to achieve advanced AI at and beyond the level of human intelligence. It is likely that we will have a few false starts (as we have already) and some over-hyped and over-stated abilities that eventually prove to be exaggerations or false claims. This is normal with such a fast-paced technology, but we must hold ourselves to the highest standards and avoid as much as possible the claims without the scrutiny of third-party peer review and examination.

Part of this challenge is due to the fact that we don't have an industry standard to measure intelligence. Alan Turing attempted to do this with his Turing Test, but the complexities of intelligence in all its forms required a much deeper and more robust scale of measurement. DeepMind have recently shared their attempt to do this, but even this doesn't do justice to the multiple aspects of intelligent capabilities.

I have previously defined my own way to measure the levels of intelligence, referred to as the Index of Intelligence, which I have summarized in the Appendix.

In this chapter we will explore further some of the trends, challenges and opportunities that will direct the future of AI research and development over the coming years and shape the roles and career options of those looking to explore ways to work in the field of AI.

Emerging trends in AI

Generative AI is only the tip of the iceberg; we have so much more in terms of foundational work to be done, more advances in learning algorithms, more complex architectures, more diversity in neuron models, more innovation on training, testing, deployment and monitoring of model performance. We have whole areas of intelligence that need significantly more investment, research and development effort. New data management approaches to better support data privacy and trust will require advances in incremental learning and unlearning. New infrastructure layers to support AI safety, audit, control and governance will likely become part of the standard framework and toolset available to data scientists – more AI innovation over the next few years than we have seen in the past five to ten years.

However, there are other technologies that empower and support the AI juggernaut, including quantum, IoT, edge computing and 5G mobile connectivity. These will all open up new applications, infrastructures and business models as well as many new AI start-ups.

Some of those start-ups are focused on using the technology to help solve some of our most important and potentially extinction-level problems, such as food security, climate change, green energy, healthcare and financial poverty. These grand challenges could save humanity from itself and fix the most urgent and complex problems we will face this century.

The path to artificial general intelligence

The work being done in both the research and applied areas of AI will move us along the path towards artificial general intelligence, but there is much debate and disagreement on how and when this will truly happen. I believe we will see a few false starts and some incorrect claims of AGI achievement. Ideally, these will need to be managed properly, with expert peer review before any such claims are shared with the mainstream media to reduce hype and negative effects of claims being shown to be false later. However, it is unlikely this will happen; instead the commercial opportunity and desire to be first past the post will be too tempting for people.

Opinions are widely separated on when AGI might be achieved, from this decade to hundreds if not a thousand years' time. The fact is we don't know, and recent developments have accelerated the field, but we know there is still much to be done before we get anywhere close to AGI capabilities.

The path towards AGI could follow a number of different routes based on the various fundamental theories of AI and how they may need to come together to form a *unified theory of AI* (which is yet to be defined). A unified theory of AI has not been discussed in the industry as yet, only multi-modal models that would be a step in the right direction but only an attempt to have a richer understanding of the world by taking in multiple sensory information.

Ethical and societal considerations

With such a disruptive technology, the biggest concern we should all have is about the impact on society. The future of the workplace is going to change dramatically, with most roles being augmented by AI-powered digital assistants and other roles significantly impacted if not removed. Obviously, we will also see many new roles and demands for data scientists and other AI roles increasing, but those whose roles are displaced may be unable to retrain and reskill to find a new job quickly.

How quickly this disruption occurs, and how governments react to help reduce the impact and support those directly affected, will be a watershed moment and likely to determine how the general population will accept this new technology era. Some have called for a universal standard income to help deal with this problem; however, trials of this approach have been tested in other countries with limited success.[4]

I also see the need for the educational system to adapt to AI. We have seen how ChatGPT in the classroom has divided opinion with educators, some encouraging children to use it while others have banned its use. But this is only a distraction from what needs to happen in the educational sector.

Firstly, AI can be used to improve educational outcomes, providing personalized teaching materials for each student based on learning performance. This can improve the speed of understanding by focusing on areas of need. AI in the classroom for this purpose is already starting to happen, but it's not widespread or part of the national curriculum.

AI is also disrupting the future of work and the needs of our future workforce. Many labour-intensive jobs will be partially or fully automated via mechanical robots controlled by AI. We need more knowledge workers, more knowledgeable and skilled with technology both to use it and help build it.

Ethical considerations are wide-ranging and important to deliver responsible and trustworthy AI applications. More needs to be done to ensure every company has a set of core AI principles that cover the ethical considerations. Various institutions and companies have published ethical frameworks that can serve as a good starting point, but each firm needs to determine its own approach and priorities here.

I believe as the industry matures, more standardization, together with practical tools and frameworks, will emerge to support ethical best practices across industries and overall, from a country perspective.

The evolution of AI careers

The roles available within the AI sector are varied and fast evolving. The main role we see today, that of a data scientist, was first introduced widely only in 2008.[5] A more recent example of a new role in the world of AI is that of prompt engineer, new in 2023 and directly related to the introduction of ChatGPT (a combination of generative and conversational AI).

There are many other roles, both technical and non-technical, needed for a successful AI and ML team, from ML engineers and MLOps to data engineers as well as the more traditional IT roles such as full-stack developers and UX designers. Data science pods or Agile teams will typically include all of these roles as well as some or all of scrum master, product owner and business analyst.

We have also seen other roles, including data labeller, ethics and governance officer and chief AI officer. Within each role there will be levels of responsibility; for example, with data science, you might start as a junior, then over time and with experience move to senior, lead and eventually head data scientist. The role may then expand to lead several teams at a group or department level and then at the country or company scale.

While the specific abilities for each of these roles will vary, each requires a level of interdisciplinary skills that span both technical and non-technical elements, including for example good communication and storytelling.

Managing a career and planning for future moves and progress, one needs to be proactive, as no one will focus as much on your career as you will and should. Don't leave it to chance and hope that things will happen. You must give yourself the best possible chance of success and advancement that you can. This includes keeping up to date with the latest advances in technology and development processes, and investing in time and effort to train yourself up on these new aspects.

CAREER TIP: One of the best ways I have engineered career progression is to make sure I help solve problems for my manager. For example, one time I knew one of my colleagues was about to hand in his notice to leave the team. I could see this left my manager a problem regarding whom that person would hand over his responsibilities and application ownership to – well, it was an obvious way for me to expand my own platform, and so I immediately volunteered myself to help do the handover and take over his responsibilities.

CAREER TIP: As technology moves so fast, I would take a week's holiday which I called my Geek Week. This was an opportunity for me to get away from my day-to-day work and focus on learning new technologies, techniques and languages that I wanted to understand but had limited opportunities within my job at that moment in time. This served me well over the years and allowed me to keep my development skills blade sharp.

Research and innovation

Globally there are more AI researchers and AI start-ups than we have ever seen before – well over 300,000 researchers in both universities and large tech companies[6] and over 67,000 companies[7] using or developing AI.

Our expectations for AI are so much higher than for our own mental abilities; we demand AI be as close to perfect as possible, if not completely infallible. For example, with self-driving cars, even if on average we can show that they are much safer than human drivers, we are instantly concerned if we see one accident caused by AI automation. Almost perfect is not good enough for some applications.

We also require our AI to be able to explain its decisions, with decision transparency and explainability a requirement not only for regulated industries such as financial and medical, but also for other decision making. This will become increasingly important as the decisions our AI makes, via recommendations, may become less obvious to us as its deep insights and knowledge extend far beyond our own human abilities.

While generative AI has made the mainstream for text and images/videos, we will see deeper applications with it having more creative outputs. I certainly believe the first movie fully created by AI, from the script to the characters, the sets and camera angles, the music and soundtrack will soon be released. But much more than this, generative AI will soon create new products, make new discoveries. In 2024, DeepMind released an AI model that had specified over 380,000 new stable materials.[8] This is going to be a massive area of growth and will dramatically accelerate the entire scientific sector, potentially moving us far past exponential growth to a level that we will struggle to keep up with.

Academia has always been a significant powerhouse in the advancement of AI; however, this seems to have somewhat changed in recent years. The big tech firms have invested billions of dollars to build research teams that rival the research done at universities. Many professors have a foot in both camps, wanting to stay aligned with a university but also keen to exploit the benefits of commercial applications. This has historically been somewhat cyclical, driven by the funding available and commercial interest, with previous AI winters reducing the interest and driving the sector back to pure academic endeavours.

While formal education isn't for everyone, getting a base foundation of education in such a far-reaching topic is not such a bad idea if you have time and money to do so. This will prove valuable to you and give you both the broad and deep perspectives that are important in such a fast-paced environment.

The future of work

It is clear that the way we work is changing, as the need for more remote working has accelerated the onboarding of cloud-based applications and other technologies, so much so that some firms are now operating in fully remote mode. This may in the first instance seem unrelated to AI, but you would be very much mistaken. Remote working leads to increased isolation. This in turn opens the door for digital assistants to provide advice and guidance to employees on a wide range of matters, from HR policy to mental health, but mostly supporting with tasks that can easily be automated. In the near future, all of our roles will be augmented with AI-powered digital assistants that can automate the mundane and provide the heavy lifting on many of your repetitive tasks.

This is as true for the role of data scientist as it is for a Java developer or for a medical doctor or a teacher. Every role in every industry will have an AI agent to help.

The role of data scientist will evolve as so much of the guesswork and trial and error involved will be automated (we already have simple versions of this with AutoML) for example. The role will be more focused on understanding the business problem, working with the technology and assistants to best solve it and then showcasing the results in the best way to communicate the benefits.

Building technology of all types will be a very different professional activity to that of today and yesterday. Faster and better shall be the tech industry motto.

Challenges and uncertainties

The world of AI has changed so much in my lifetime, it is difficult to know exactly where it will go and what will be achieved in the next 20 to 30 years, especially as technology is now advancing at such an exponential rate. Expert opinion is widely divided on when AGI will be achieved or whether it is even possible. Many think that it is impossible to emulate intelligence on a non-carbon-based substrate, or that consciousness is more than just the atoms, molecules, and electrical and chemical signals within our brains.

This is why, fundamentally, the field is so intriguing and complex. We have so many unanswered questions, and while we have now started to build AI that can solve real-world problems for us, we are still a million miles (or more) away from building the superintelligence that is the ultimate moonshot for the industry and has the potential to unlock our utopian future.

For me, this makes working in the field of AI so much more attractive, with so many innovations and discoveries waiting to be found. History has shown us many times that these types of impactful discoveries can be surfaced by anyone, regardless of where you work and what you do – the landscape is rich with buried AI treasure just waiting for someone to dig it up. It could be you.

The next AI winter (or ice age)

While it is very easy to be overly optimistic right now, we should try to learn the lessons from history. As an industry, we have already had two previous AI winters, the definition of an AI winter being a significant reduction of interest in the field from investors, practitioners and researchers. It's essentially a cooling off from the field for a period of time due to disappointment in results and achievements. This cycle of interest is typical in many fields, not just AI.

It is possible, with the monumental hype and investment gravitating towards all things generative AI at the moment, that we are seeing the start of the next AI winter cycle. Will the realization that generative AI will not deliver AGI be the trigger that starts the freeze?

It is certain that investment will eventually cool off, and that the amazing progress we've seen recently may be more difficult to equal or better in the near future. But hopefully, the fact that AI is now delivering real-world practical benefits will be the deciding fact that will avert us from a third AI winter. As I wrote in a recent article, 'we may not be able to stave off a machine learning AI winter; perhaps it's an inevitable cycle. But to stave off an even worse and very, very destructive AI Ice Age, we need to widen the focus and get AGI back on its feet.'

AN AI WINTER MAY BE INEVITABLE. WHAT WE SHOULD FEAR MORE: AN AI ICE AGE[9]

In *The Queen's Gambit*, the Netflix drama about a chess genius, the main character is incredibly focused and driven. You might even say machine-like. Perhaps you could go so far as to say she's a little bit like an incredibly single-minded AI program like AlphaGo.

Hoping not to give any spoilers here, but in the drama, Beth eventually succeeds *not* just because she's a chess prodigy, able to see the board many moves ahead. She succeeds because she teams up with fellow players who give her hints and tips on the psychology and habits of her main 'Big Boss' opponent.

In other words, she employs tactics, strategy, reasoning and planning; she sees more than the board. She reads the room, one might say. Emotions play a huge part in all she does and are key to her eventual triumph in Moscow.

And this is why we're potentially in a lot of trouble with AI. AlphaGo can't do any of what Beth and her friends do. It's a brilliant bit of software, but it's an *idiot savant* – all it knows is Go.

Right now, very few people care about that. Which is why I fear we may be headed not just into another AI winter, but an almost endless AI Ice Age, perhaps decades of rejection of the approach, all the VC money taps being turned off, lack of university research funding – all the things we saw in the first AI winter of 1974–80 and the second of 1987–93.

Only much, much worse.

Moore's Law continues to be our friend, but even that has limits

I'm also convinced that the only way to save the amazing achievements we've seen with programs like AlphaGo is to make them more like Beth – able to 'see' much, much more than just 'the board' in front of them.

Let's put all this in context. Right now, we are without doubt enjoying the best period AI has ever had. Years and years of hard backroom slog at the theoretical level have been accompanied by superb improvements in hardware performance – a combination that raised our game really without us asking. Hence today's undoubted AI success story: machine learning. Everyone is betting on this approach and its roots in deep learning and big data, which is fine; genuine progress and real applications are being delivered at the moment.

But there's a hard stop coming. One of the inherent issues for deep learning that is you need bigger and bigger neural networks and parameters to achieve more than you did last time, and so you soon end up with incredible numbers of parameters: the full version of GPT-3 has 175 billion. But to train those sizes of networks takes immense computational power – and even though Moore's Law continues to be our friend, even that has limits. And we're set to reach them a lot sooner than many would like to think.

Despite its reputation for handwaving and love of unobtainium, the AI field is full of realists. Most have painful memories of what happened the last time AI's promise met intractable reality, a cycle which gives rise to the concept of the 'AI winter'. In the UK, in 1973 a scathing analysis – the infamous Lighthill Report – concluded that AI just wasn't worth putting any more money into. Similarly fed up, once amazingly generous Defence paymasters in the US ended the first heuristic search-based boom, and the field went into steep decline until the expert systems/knowledge engineering explosion of the 1980s, which also, eventually, went 'cold' when too many over-egged promises met the real world.

To be clear, both periods provided incredible advances,

including systems that saved money for people and improved industries. AI never goes away, either; anyone working in IT knows that there's always advanced programming and smart systems somewhere helping out – we don't even call them AI anymore, they just work without issue. So on one hand, AI won't stop, even if it goes out of fashion once again; getting computers and robots to help us is just too useful an endeavour to stop.

What we need is smart systems that are better at more than one 'thing'

But what *will* happen is an AI winter that will follow today's boom. Sometime soon, data science will stop being fashionable; ML models will stop being trusted; entrepreneurs offering the City a deep learning solution to financial problem X won't have their emails returned.

And what *might* well happen beyond that is even worse… not just a short period of withdrawal of interest, but a deep, deep freeze – 10, 20, 30 years long. I don't want to see that happen, and that's just not because I love AI or want my very own HAL 9000 (though, of course I do – so do you). I don't want to see it happen because I know that artificial intelligence is real, and while there may be genuinely fascinating philosophical arguments for and against it, eventually we will create something that can do things as well as humans can.

But note that I said 'things'. AlphaGo is better than all of us (certainly me) at playing games. Google Translate is better than me at translating multiple languages, and so on. What we need are smart systems that are better at more than one 'thing'… that can start being intelligent, even at very low levels, outside a very narrow domain. Step forward AGI, *Artificial General Intelligence*, which are suites of programs that apply intelligence to a wide variety of problems, in much the same ways humans can.

We're only seeing the most progress in learning because that's where all the investment is going

For example, we've only been focused on *learning* in the last 15 years. But AI done properly needs to cover a range of intelligence capabilities, of which being able to learn and spot patterns is just one; there's reasoning, there's understanding, there's a lot of other types of intelligence capabilities that should be part of an overall artificial intelligence practice or capability.

We know why that is – we're focused on learning because we got good traction with that and made solid progress. But there's all the other AI capabilities that we should be also looking at and investigating, and we're just not. It's a Catch-22: all the smart money is going into machine learning because that's where we're seeing the most progress, but we're only seeing the most progress in learning because that's where all the investment is going!

To sum up, then: we may not be able to stave off a machine learning AI winter; perhaps it's an inevitable cycle. But to stave off an even worse and very, very destructive AI Ice Age, I think we need to widen the focus here, get AGI back on its feet, and help our 'Beths' get better at a lot more than just 'chess' … or we're just going to see them turned off, one by one.

Final thoughts – the road ahead

The AI landscape for the next five to ten years will be full of opportunities, new roles, new approaches, new technologies and new intelligent abilities. But it's not just on the data science side that opportunities will be bountiful; the core infrastructure will evolve significantly, as will the data management, privacy and data trust requirements. New approaches like distributed, federated and quantum computing will change the methodologies and processes to build AI. Other technologies, such as Web 3 and the metaverse will become more mass market and again alter the landscape in how AI is utilized.

Robotics is also an area of rapid development; controlled by AI, we will see a flood of robots to assist with a wide range of manual labour tasks. Android-formed robots are already in development from Tesla (called Optimus),[10] Boston Dynamics (called Atlas)[11] and others. Again this related field will open up many new career opportunities, both within AI and with robotics.

And no doubt there will be new technologies that haven't even been imagined yet that will enter the ecosystem and change the game.

Ultimately, throughout your career you will have to have a lifetime of learning and change direction as your experience and knowledge grow. Finding the best role for you at any given time will create your unique career path and define who you will become in the future. This journey is the most exciting part of anyone's working life, and it will be full of surprises, twists and turns that will provide you with the ongoing challenges and aspirations you will need in your working life.

AI can be considered as being the most advanced technology available at any time, and this partly explains why it is difficult to define what AI is, as over the decades it has changed and will continue to do so in the future. But being on the frontier of technology developments is always exciting and challenging and has provided many with a substantially rewarding career.

In this chapter we have discussed some of the latest elements of AI research and development, together with some of the related technologies that will shape the future progress and achievements we will see in the coming years for advanced AI and AGI.

Notes

1 Gov.uk (2023) Countries agree to safe and responsible development of frontier AI in landmark Bletchley Declaration, www.gov.uk/government/news/countries-agree-to-safe-and-responsible-development-of-frontier-ai-in-landmark-bletchley-declaration (archived at https://perma.cc/6TM6-QU9E)

2   Baumann, O (2023) How much energy do we expend using our brains? Bond University, bond.edu.au/news/how-much-energy-do-we-expend-using-our-brains (archived at https://perma.cc/3XA7-8XMJ)

3   Sreedhar, N (2023) AI and its carbon footprint: How much water does ChatGPT consume? Mint Lounge, lifestyle.livemint.com/news/big-story/ai-carbon-footprint-openai-chatgpt-water-google-microsoft-111697802189371.html (archived at https://perma.cc/3YH9-VENF)

4   Universal basic income, en.wikipedia.org/wiki/Universal_basic_income (archived at https://perma.cc/Y53C-YN2E)

5   Botelho, B (2022) Definition data scientist, Tech Target, www.techtarget.com/searchenterpriseai/definition/data-scientist (archived at https://perma.cc/L2P8-CHED)

6   MMC (2019) The State of AI: Divergence, Chapter 6: The war for talent, www.stateofai2019.com/chapter-6-the-war-for-talent (archived at https://perma.cc/LY2C-H4B5)

7   Duarte, F (2024) How many AI companies are there? Exploding Topics, explodingtopics.com/blog/number-ai-companies# (archived at https://perma.cc/M9XV-H2S4)

8   Merchant, A and Cubuk, E D (2023) Millions of new materials discovered with deep learning, Deepmind, deepmind.google/discover/blog/millions-of-new-materials-discovered-with-deep-learning/ (archived at https://perma.cc/KZJ6-A9YR)

9   Pardoe, A (2021) An AI winter may be inevitable. What we should fear more: an AI Ice Age, pardoe.ai/blog/an-ai-winter-may-be-inevitable-what-we-should-fear-more-an-ai-ice-age/ (archived at https://perma.cc/GN82-APUF)

10   McCallum, S (2022) Tesla boss Elon Musk presents humanoid robot Optimus, BBC, www.bbc.co.uk/news/technology-63100636 (archived at https://perma.cc/LV2U-BBFJ)

11   Boston Dynamics (nd) Atlas® and beyond: the world's most dynamic robots, bostondynamics.com/atlas/ (archived at https://perma.cc/J8QG-944P)

PART TWO

The technology

Artificial intelligence is not just one technology, it's a collection of many varied techniques across a range of different methodologies. It is also a reference to our most advanced technologies, evolving all the time, as we look to build more intelligent technology that can help us solve more challenging problems.

As the technology advances, understanding the full range of available approaches is one of the main challenges for a modern data scientist. Machine learning is just one area of the field; the true potential of AI will only be realized from the fusion of many techniques and approaches.

Developing AI-based solutions for the most complex problems is also challenging because of the large range of options available. Much of the art and skill of a data scientist is being able to know instinctively the right type of AI or ML to best solve any given problem – and this only really comes with experience.

We are also in a tremendously fast-moving period, with research and applied development at a level of capacity never seen before; what is breakthrough technology today will be legacy in a matter of months or even weeks. Keeping up with all this change is challenging; building solutions that stand the test of time is also impossible, requiring continued improvements as new abilities surface.

CHAPTER FIVE

Understanding AI

Overview

The term artificial intelligence encompasses the entire field of study to produce intelligent capabilities. It covers many areas of expertise, from computer science and neuroscience, to mathematics, philosophy, psychology and even physics. It has also produced, over the last 70 years, many different methodologies, theories, techniques and technologies. The industry has experienced waves of interest in the subject, with the troughs known as AI winters. The research and development of AI is currently at an all-time high, with new research papers being published weekly on new algorithms and architectures. From decade to decade, what is considered the most advanced type of AI changes, and now we see much faster advances, at an exponential rate of change and beyond. But this can be bad, leading to a blinkered mindset to the development of the technology, with the industry getting obsessed with one sub-field or technique, forgetting that true intelligence will require a range of intelligent capabilities. The previous AI winters have shown us that we have a tendency to put all our faith in one approach until we realize its limitations and issues cannot be solved without taking a much broader perspective.

The history of AI

The history of AI can be traced back to the 1950s when researchers first began exploring the idea of creating machines that could perform tasks that would normally require human intelligence.

The Dartmouth Conference in 1956 is widely considered as the birthplace of AI. Researchers gathered to discuss the possibility of building machines that could perform tasks that normally require human intelligence, such as understanding natural language, recognizing objects and solving problems.

In the 1960s the first AI programs were developed, including John McCarthy's Logic Theorist and Herbert Simon's General Problem Solver. These programs were able to perform simple tasks, such as solving mathematical problems, playing games and translating languages.

However, in 1966 the first AI winter (a term used to indicate a period of cooling off or slowdown in the AI industry) began as a consequence of overstated expectations and the resulting underfunding. Despite the early successes, researchers were unable to develop machines that could perform more complex tasks, leading to a decrease in funding and a slowdown in progress.

Then in the 1970s, AI experienced a resurgence, with the development of expert systems that were able to perform specific tasks that normally require human expertise, such as diagnosing diseases, recommending treatments and making financial predictions.

Our second AI winter began in the late 1980s due to a combination of overstated expectations and the lack of progress in developing truly intelligent machines. Funding for AI research decreased, and many researchers left the field.

In the mid to late 1990s, we experienced another resurgence with the development of machine learning algorithms, such as decision trees, neural networks and support vector machines, which allowed machines to learn from data and improve their performance over time.

Then in 1997, a chess match between Deep Blue and Garry Kasparov took place, with Deep Blue, an AI system developed by IBM, defeating the world chess champion. This marked a significant milestone in the development of AI, demonstrating the ability of machines to perform tasks that require human-level intelligence.

This started another wave of enthusiasm in the 2010s with the advance of deep learning algorithms, which allowed machines to learn and make predictions based on large amounts of data. These algorithms have been used to achieve state-of-the-art results in tasks such as image and speech recognition, natural language processing and autonomous driving – and are able for the first time in our history to show performance better than humans at specific tasks.

Today, AI is being used in a wide range of applications, from healthcare to finance, and is playing an increasingly important role in our daily lives. Despite this progress, the development of truly intelligent machines remains a challenge, and AI continues to be an active area of research and development.

The history of AI is marked by periods of rapid progress followed by AI winters. Many experts in the field believe we are heading towards another AI winter, with the current overestimation of the abilities of deep learning and large language models, and the significant costs of building such deep models becoming a major barrier to entry.

How the industry matures and expands over the next few years will be critical to longer-term success and the avoidance of a third AI winter.

A more detailed timeline of key AI milestones

Below are some of the key milestones in the journey to AI from its early beginnings. This is not a definitive list of events over the last 70 years or so, but it will give you a flavour of the significant amount of work that has happened over many decades to get us to where we are now. We still have much more to do, but we are already standing on the shoulders of giants with what has come before us:

1943: Warren McCulloch and Walter Pitts develop the first artificial neural network, which is inspired by the structure of the human brain and is able to learn and adapt to new data.

1950: Alan Turing proposes the Turing Test, a measure of a machine's ability to exhibit intelligent behaviour equivalent to, or indistinguishable from, that of a human.

1956: John McCarthy coins the term 'artificial intelligence' and organizes the Dartmouth Conference, where the field of AI is founded.

1966: Joseph Weizenbaum creates ELIZA, one of the first natural language processing programs.

1970s: AI research focuses on the development of expert systems, which are able to perform tasks such as medical diagnosis and financial forecasting with a high degree of accuracy.

1980s: Researchers develop machine learning algorithms, which allow computers to learn from data without being explicitly programmed.

1990s: The internet and the availability of large amounts of data drive a resurgence of interest and funding in AI research.

2002: The DARPA Grand Challenge, a competition for autonomous vehicles, is held for the first time.

2005: IBM's Deep Blue computer defeats world chess champion Garry Kasparov, marking the first time a computer has defeated an expert human at chess.

2010: Apple introduces Siri, a virtual personal assistant that uses natural language processing to understand and respond to voice commands.

2011: IBM's Watson computer defeats two human champions on the game show *Jeopardy!*, demonstrating the capabilities of machine learning and natural language processing.

2014: Google DeepMind's AlphaGo defeats the world champion at the board game Go, a game that is considered much more complex than chess.

2015: Tesla releases its first self-driving car, the Tesla Autopilot.

2016: Google DeepMind's AlphaGo defeats the world's top Go player again, this time using a more advanced version of the algorithm.

2018: Google announces that its DeepMind AI system has achieved 'superhuman' performance at a number of Atari 2600 video games.

2020: OpenAI's GPT-3, a language-generation AI model, is released. It is one of the largest and most advanced language models to date, with 175 billion parameters.

2022: ChatGPT is released and causes huge interest from the public in these generative AIs (both conversational AI and image and video generation).

2023: The large tech companies are embracing generative and conversational AI to enhance their products and services, including reinventing internet search.

2024: The maturity of generative AI technologies continues, with many more businesses looking to implement AI to gain productivity benefits.

Innovation at the speed of thought

The landscape is changing, faster than we have ever seen before. We are all having to adapt to this dynamic environment. This is challenging for companies who have previously done business the same way for decades. Embracing the digital native world will be too difficult for some and they will ultimately fail.

We discovered electricity in the 1700s but took us 200 years to truly master its application. Artificial intelligence was first conceived in the 1950s and the technology is still very much in its infancy. Given the exponential acceleration of technology advancement, defined by the World Economic Forum as the Fourth Industrial Revolution, it becomes almost impossible for us to imagine what our world will look like 30 or 40 years from now.

All industry will undoubtedly change dramatically in the coming years, and while it will be empowered by the capabilities being created by the thousands of AI researchers and developers working around the world, it will be focused on the customer experience required by the younger generations of customers who are by default digital natives and have very different requirements to previous generations.

It will be very interesting to see how industry reacts to this changing landscape; who the winners and losers will be in this new competitive environment is for now difficult to see.

Overview of AI

Now follows a very abbreviated introduction to the different forms of artificial intelligence. We must start with the eight pillars of AI, which are the capabilities of understanding, knowledge representation, reasoning, learning, planning, common sense, creativity and solving. These are the main areas of AI, which can easily be forgotten as focus in one of the areas can dominate, as at the moment with machine learning methods.

Expert systems, rule-based systems and decision trees

One of the earlier methods of AI was termed expert systems. Often expert systems were also known as rule-based systems.

They initially relied on extracting knowledge from domain experts in the form of observation, interviews and surveys, then encoding that knowledge as rules into an expert system that could be used as a substitute for that expert on the particular process or workflow in question.

The problem with these systems was that it was challenging to extract all the intrinsic knowledge from the expert, especially all the fringe/edge cases. In some cases, the experts didn't want to share all of their knowledge, as they feared for their own jobs. Another problem with these rule-based systems was that over time the number of rules became excessively large and potentially challenging to maintain, even producing conflicts between rules. These problems required supporting methods to help prune the rules and highlight potential overlap and conflict.

Modern versions of these expert systems are called decision trees and they now use data directly to define the rules. Decision trees are a very useful machine learning technique with explainability and decision transparency built in as default. This allows the exact rules that have been used for a specific decision to be easily determined.

Knowledge representation

Knowledge-based systems are methods to store extracted information and knowledge. The most recent and popular type of knowledge base is that of a graph database. Here the knowledge is stored in the form of triples (subject-predicate-object), often called a knowledge graph, as you can have a single subject with multiple predicates. This is often used to represent knowledge of relationships between entities extracted from other data or information. Such KBs or graphs allow the embedded knowledge to be searched using easy-to-understand queries.

Machine learning

All machine learning methods utilize data to learn, referred to as training data. The skill is selecting the correct machine learning method as well as the right subset of data to use as its training data to achieve the desired outcome.

There is a huge diversity of methods, inspired by different areas, from mathematics, probabilities and statistics, to cognitive and evolutionary understanding.

Mathematics, and specifically statistics, has been a key element of many AI techniques; leveraging the concepts of probabilities, these methods provide some of the fundamental building blocks for intelligence capabilities.

Mathematical methods (other than statistics) include support vector machines, sparse dictionaries and rule-based methods (association rule learning/inductive logic programming/similarity and metric learning).

Biologically inspired methods include both cognitive methods (including neural networks, deep learning and hierarchical temporal memory) and evolutionary methods (agent-based and genetic algorithms).

We then come to some of the most advanced methods that have shown significant promise in recent years, including deep learning and reinforcement learning.

Deep learning

In the last few years, a method called deep learning has become most interesting to the research community. This is a form of machine learning, specifically neural networks, which leverages more complex topologies and number of layers of neurons. Two main forms of deep learning have become popular, one called convolutional neural networks (CNN) and the other recurrent neural networks (RNN). Fundamentally, the first is good at image analysis and object detection, the other is good at language processing.

Reinforcement learning

This is actually a training algorithm that allows feedback from the environment to influence the learning, ensuring that positive outcomes in the environment (like increasing the score in a game) are rewarded by increased learning of the action that resulted in that outcome. This approach seems to replicate in simplistic form the way humans learn, by trial and error, getting feedback from the external environment as a method of measuring success.

Other techniques

There are many other AI techniques, which is actually part of the challenge for data scientists building models for intelligence applications. With so many techniques available, part of the skill of building an intelligence system is the correct selection of the AI technique to solve the problem with the required level of performance, matching the complexity of the problem with the complexity of the solution.

The landscape of techniques is also changing fast; there are thousands of researchers both academic and commercial publishing papers every week with advances in methods and techniques, pushing the boundaries of both the theory and application of artificial intelligence. This is a very exciting time for those involved in this field of study, but there is a real challenge to keep up with the latest advances.

The beauty of intelligence and the human brain

It seems safe to say that there is extraordinary complexity within the human brain, and at many different levels. There are 100 billion neurons and up to 1,000 trillion synaptic connections in the average human brain. From the diversity of the neurons themselves, their topologies and functioning give rise to a multitude of variations to the structural layering and hierarchy within different parts of the brain. No doubt it is the most complex machine ever constructed. We are only starting to understand how it works.

Add the dynamic nature of how it learns, growing connections between neurons, altering the weight of the connections as it constantly learns and adapts, new neurons replacing old neurons. Watching this process actually happen makes you realize the true beauty of intelligence and recognize that our mind is the most treasured object in the universe.

If you ever needed motivation to study a subject, recognizing that intelligence is created by the most beautiful and complex object in the universe must surely help!

It is clear that the minds of animals and humans have incrementally developed and advanced from the benefits of evolution over time. Some animals show very similar cognitive capabilities to those of humans while others have distinctly different arrangements and structures but still demonstrate a relatively high quality of intelligence.

Taking advantage of the evolutionary design of natural intelligence will no doubt help us to produce more capable artificial intelligence. Understanding how the human brain works must certainly advance our knowledge of how to build advanced AI systems, and even if we do not follow the design of the human brain precisely, it certainly must serve as a very good guide for us to learn from. We can consider it as a blueprint for intelligence.

Artificial general intelligence

With the recent developments of generative AI and large language models (LLMs) we are starting to see the move from narrow to more general AI capabilities. Having a single tool that can be used on a range of different applications (from writing marketing materials to passing exams to creating coding) certainly feels like an example of general intelligence.

Some have even speculated that the best LLMs are starting to demonstrate emergent properties of intelligence (such as understanding and reasoning). However, many other experts have emphasized that the LLMs are simply stochastic parrots, prone to error and hallucinations.

While the capabilities of ChatGPT and other similar generative and conversational AI have amazed the world (over 100 million users signed up to use ChatGPT within the first month of it being available publicly), its true level of intelligence is highly questionable.

Many knowledgeable experts in the field believe that LLMs are not the solution for true language understanding. Others, including myself, think that AGI will be produced with a fusion of many different AI techniques and methods.

Reflecting on the complexity we know about within the brains of animals and humans, it would suggest we need significantly higher sophistication in our architectures and learning paradigms.

There are so many aspects to intelligence that we have not been able to replicate yet – reasoning with explanation, planning and solving, common sense, self-awareness, creativity and emotions. Our attempts so far have only been able to imitate our own responses without any independent cognitive capabilities.

This is a major obstacle that will be both controversial and challenging for the industry to develop and overcome in the coming years and decades.

Superintelligence and the singularity

Once AGI is achieved, and we have a single entity that has levels of intelligence across multiple (if not all) subjects beyond that of the collective intelligence of humans, we enter another major milestone in human and intelligence evolution.

Superintelligence will embody a level of intelligence we won't have experienced before and potentially will be unable to comprehend. It is possible that it will construct suggestions to help us solve a given problem that, to us, has no clear solution.

This situation will become very uncomfortable for humans – having an artificially intelligent agent so smart that its suggestions for us, while most likely to be correct, are difficult if not impossible to comprehend. How we decide to trust this superintelligent agent will define us.

Superintelligence will also be knowledgeable on artificial intelligence, so much so that it would be able to invent new versions of itself, continuing to improve itself and further push its intelligence forward. This would create generation after generation of new versions of superintelligent AI systems – this self-creation of technology is termed the singularity. This could produce an AI system that the best AI researchers in the world do not understand.

How our relationship with technology, especially artificial intelligence, progresses over the next few decades will potentially shape our own human evolution. We will need to decide how to utilize the benefits available with such power without exposing ourselves to some of the risks and challenges.

Measuring intelligence

One of the challenges we face as an industry is twofold. Firstly, we need a solid definition of artificial intelligence. This may sound like an odd situation for the AI industry to be in, given that the technology is 70 years old. We can of course leverage the original definition that John McCarthy gave when he first coined the term back in 1956. This is not a bad place to start, but the field has progressed and several experts have slightly differing variations of this definition. Ultimately, the similarities are greater than the differences and so this is a somewhat academic point. The second point, and more importantly, is that we need to understand how we can accurately measure the level of intelligence achieved by any form of artificial intelligence.

Yes, we have IQ and other subject-level tests for humans, and Alan Turing devised his Turing Test for AI, which is still a valid starting point, but this misses the complexities and range of capabilities that constitute intelligence that it would be useful for us to quantify as we progress to build more advanced forms of AI.

While others have proposed a scale of AI, from basic narrow AI to AGI and superintelligence, the details and approach to measurement are lacking. It is for this reason I have developed what I call the Index of Intelligence. This index (detailed in the Appendix) provides a sliding scale of intelligent ability across a full range of intelligence capabilities. This will help the industry to have a global benchmark for comparison and avoid any false statements or over-hyping of future models and AI systems.

Recent advances

One of the reasons I was so interested and motivated to learn about AI at the start of my career was my realization that AI simply meant the most advanced form of technology. This statement has been evidenced over the last few decades, as what is considered the cutting edge of AI development changes over time. No more real has this been than over the last few years.

The combination of generative AI (based on the foundation of the technique known as the Transformer) and conversational AI (leveraging reinforcement learning) produced the capabilities demonstrated by OpenAI in November 2022 with its release of ChatGPT. This took the world by storm, and for the first time illustrated a general-purpose AI, able to perform a range of tasks, from writing poetry to constructing programming code.

While the initial release was impressive, the big tech firms could see its potential and raced to integrate it into their product suites. The firms with search engines wanted to enable a more interactive search, allowing better filtering to be determined via a conversational interface. Other firms saw the potential of better customer support chatbots and personal assistants. Additional major functions included productivity gains within knowledge worker tools.

However, this was just the start of the race to build upon such a strong foundational capability. While the results from these LLMs are impressive, they still only provide relatively generic output, which led to the realization of the skills needed to provide well-formed and context-sensitive prompts. So much so that the role of prompt engineer was born, and a mass of prompt cheat sheets for different purposes flooded the internet.

Everyone was looking how to integrate generative AI into their applications and services to provide these cutting-edge abilities. However, it soon became clear that for many real-world applications the LLMs needed more information to improve the quality and precision of responses. Quickly, co-pilots, orchestration and chaining technologies were layered on top of the LLMs, together with knowledge bases of corporate information and document stores to ground the LLMs with additional context information augmenting the user prompt. This then required widening the input text window to provide more input data into the models.

Additionally, the link to external information, leveraging the huge amount of information already available in search engines, and the ability to action third-party tasks to create a platform of automation orchestrated by the conversational AI interface, both provide a major utility for exploration and exploitation by those looking to build intelligent applications.

Certainly, the AI world has been obsessed with generative AI and in particular large language models, as the real-world applications are significant and CEOs/CTOs of businesses of all sizes look to exploit the potential productivity gains from this tool.

This will continue to advance in the near future, with significant funding made to generative AI start-ups, more open-source and commercial models being trained, more focus on customized and bespoke models for specific purposes and industries. We already see the broader capability of generative, with image and video creation occurring and in other mediums too, including music, scientific discoveries and product design.

Many experts have opposing opinions on LLMs, saying that they have limited, if any, understanding or reasoning abilities, despite being able to display some degree of capability in this area. Fundamentally, LLMs are just statistical predictors of the next word in a sequence, but having been trained on huge quantities of data and with billions of internal parameters, the demonstrated outcomes are astonishing.

Focus has been to advance the performance of LLMs, reducing hallucinations and being more context-sensitive to achieve more customized results. Grounding prompts with additional information (from the enterprise knowledge base or graph) orchestrated by a co-pilot, or looking to perform refinement learning with bespoke data have been successful methods to improve the outcomes of LLMs for specific tasks.

But we must remember that AI is not just about generative – this is just one element of what AI can do. We also have to acknowledge the diversity of opinion on the true underlying intelligence within the generative models, which fundamentally goes back to the previous section on how we properly assess the level of intelligence embedded in these AI systems we build.

Final thoughts

What we consider to be AI now is vastly different to what we had in the 1980s and 1990s, and it will surely be much more advanced at the end of the 2020s and into the 2030s. What it will be, and what it might be capable of is, at this stage, anyone's guess, but we are most definitely heading towards AI that has more utility, more mass-market appeal, and will be increasingly more integrated with everything we do.

Not only should this make us more productive, but it should help us solve our most challenging issues of the day that currently put our planet and even our own existence at risk.

The fusion of human and machine is already upon us. How many of you are constantly next to your smart phone? This integration of humans and technology, each providing unique talents and skills, will be our future, leveraging the huge computational power and data processing heavy lifting of AI to allow us more detailed and knowledgeable insights.

If we can use the power of AI to make fewer mistakes, to better our future and help us navigate the challenges we face, then we must balance these benefits against any of the potential pitfalls or safety concerns. Responsible and trustworthy AI is our key to a robust and beneficial future of AI-powered humanity.

In this chapter we have provided a high-level overview of the full range of AI techniques and technologies. The field is diverse, complex and certainly at the moment fast moving, with new algorithms, innovations and research being published on a daily basis.

Keeping up to date requires everyone working in the field to dedicate themselves to continuous learning and have an inquisitive nature to explore what is happening in other parts of the AI world.

Such rapid change and advancement creates real opportunity for many to become knowledgeable in specific areas and even, if you wish, be an expert in the field.

AI is a truly exciting, empowering and disruptive set of technologies; it will change our world and our lives for the better, potentially altering the course of human evolution and, if we use it responsibly, ensuring our long-term survival as a species.

CHAPTER SIX

Overview of machine learning

Machine learning is a subfield of artificial intelligence that involves training algorithms to automatically learn and improve from data without being explicitly programmed. This is a significant departure from how we have built technology systems and applications previously and we are still discovering the best ways to do it to help us avoid things like decision bias and other ethical challenges.

This chapter introduces the basic concepts of machine learning, including common algorithms and approaches like supervised and unsupervised learning.

The basics of machine learning

Machine learning methods use two stages. The first stage is termed training and typically uses an annotated training data set in which the abstracted machine autonomously identifies associations and patterns within the data related to the desired output response (often known as the prediction). The learning process will present the training dataset to the neural network and, based on the calculated error between the desired (or target) output and the actual output, the internal parameters of the machine, i.e. the internal connection weights, are adjusted to gradually make improvements to the desired output. This process is done repeatedly over the complete dataset many times. Machine learning eliminates the need to define complex hand-crafted rules that strictly follow a defined specification written by the programmer (as occurs in the development of computer programs) since the abstract machine in ML/AI technology is not processing data on a step-by-step instructional basis, but instead uses training data to learn the logic to solve a specific problem and thereby reconfigures the machine. Machine learning does not therefore follow an 'if-then' statement approach. On a hardware abstraction level, each iteration is an emulation of a new and better structural topology defined at the end of the process and not the beginning.

Rather, the functional capability of the ANN (artificial neural network) is defined through the creation of an internal model independent of the software programmer and independent of the expression or language chosen by the software programmer. This first stage will also use a separate validation data set to help guide the training or learning process by measuring the accuracy of the partially trained model to infer the correct output for the validation dataset.

Once an ANN model is trained, it can be used in the second stage, often known as inference, to make predictions on new data presented to the model inputs. This second stage is using the trained model to generate predictions based on what it has learnt from the training dataset on new data presented to it.

The essence of training an ANN is the simulation of the structural network (topology) of a neural network, which is a highly simplified approximation of the neurons within a human brain. The method of simulation can be implemented in various ways, including hardware electronics, dedicated hardware accelerators, multi-processor hardware (like video cards) and simulation software. In all cases it is the parameters of the synaptic connections and neurons that are being altered to improve performance accuracy of the overall machine. Once effectively trained and indeed after every iteration the new intelligent machine is a better intelligent machine.

Basic structures

An ANN is made up of a collection of neurons. These neurons are arranged into a structure of layers. These layers are labelled as the input layer, hidden layer(s) and the output layer. The hidden layers are located between the input and output layers. There is typically more than one hidden layer, although in its simplest form a hidden layer is optional and the input and output layers can be directly connected. In a fully connected topology, the outputs from neurons in one layer are connected to inputs of all neurons in the next layer.

The input data is presented to the input layer neurons and the network processes this information through the neurons in each layer in turn until the output layer neurons present an output result. This process is called feed-forward.

Neurons

A neuron will take one or more inputs from the previous layer (or data inputs if in the input layer itself). For each input it will have a separate weight value (that changes during the learning process) which it applies to the input value. These weighted inputs are then aggregated together with a bias value (which may also change during the learning process). Then an activation function (in a simple example this being a sigmoid function) is used on this aggregated value to generate the neuron's output value. The neuron output value then serves as the input value from this neuron to connected neurons in the next layer of neurons.

This simple signal flow process, for both the training and prediction stages, can be performed in a computer, hardware electronics (known as digital neuromorphic hardware) and also field-programmable gate arrays (FPGAs).

Layers

A typical ANN will consist of many neurons arranged into layers. The ANN would typically have an input layer, one or more hidden layers and an output layer. It is not necessary to have the same number of neurons in each layer, and frequently that is not the case. The input data would be presented to the neurons in the input layer. In a fully connected topology, the outputs from neurons in one layer are connected to inputs of all neurons in the next layer. This data would then propagate through the input neurons and onto the neurons in the hidden layers, each neuron processing its inputs and calculating its own output. From the last hidden layer, the data will propagate to the output layer of neurons and finally the output neurons will provide the output prediction result. At each layer, the neurons will take the input data and modify it based on its internal weights to calculate that neuron's output (which is then propagated as input to the neurons in the next layer).

There are such things as 'convolutional layers' in ANNs. The simple explanation is that the input to a convolutional layer is two-dimensional, e.g. a matrix. Convolutional layers are thus able to learn 2D patterns in the input data, e.g. vertical edges in a photograph or circular shapes in the output of the previous layer.

The output layer of neurons will present a defined number of output values (often known as an output vector). As an easy-to-understand application, these outputs are used to categorize the inputs presented to them, with each output neuron representing a different category.

With some category classifications we want the network to give us the most likely (highest probability) category for the input data. A 'softmax' function is used to normalize the output values (across all output neurons), so the sum of all values in the output total to 1, and each output is between 0 and 1. Each output represents the likelihood that the input should be classified as falling within that output 'bucket'. In an effective and well-implemented ANN, this would then make the most likely category have a value close to 1 with other less likely categories having values closer to 0. So if, for example, you had an ANN trained to discriminate photographs of cats, dogs, horses and sheep, the softmax output layer would have four neurons, each associated with cat, dog, horse or sheep respectively.

The intention would be for any particular photograph to produce a value of near to 1 in one of the output neurons, and close to zero in the other three, to categorize the photograph.

In other applications, the output can be a numerical vector describing the input in an abstract manner. For example, in so-called embedding applications the network output is a multi-dimensional vector that seeks to 'describe' the input (albeit not necessarily in a human-understandable manner) such that similar inputs produce numerically similar outputs. Applying this concept to a large amount of data populates a multidimensional space with discrete data points that are associated by numerical closeness within that embedding space.

Training

For a given ANN, it will have a defined structure (network or topology), specifically the number of neurons in each layer and the number of layers. This structure will also define the total number of weights and biases from all the neurons in the network. These weights and biases are the parameters that can be changed during the training (or learning) process, and ultimately determine how the neural network responds (outputs values) to any input data that is presented to it.

The training stage aims to alter the internal parameters of the neural network. This will use an iterative learning process to determine the changes to these parameters. The learning process will use a training dataset, a validation dataset and a loss (or cost) function. It will repeatedly present the training dataset to the ANN and determine how to modify the network parameters to reduce the error in its classification (predicted output).

The job of the loss function is to determine the difference (or error) between the desired outputs (often called targets) and the actual output generated by the network. The learning process will then proportionally use this error to make small changes to the network parameters. This process is done repeatedly for every example in the training dataset. One very common approach is called back-propagation. It may use a mean squared error (MSE) loss function although other loss functions can be used with back-propagation, including cross-entropy. Cross-entropy has been found to be highly effective for category classification problems. The loss function is simply a measure of the difference between the network output and the desired output.

One cycle of the training dataset is called an epoch. After a number of epochs, the validation dataset is presented to the network and the error between the targets and actual outputs calculated. As the learning process continues, we can see how the error is reducing for the validation dataset. This is used to monitor the progress of the learning and to help determine when to stop the learning process. The validation dataset is not used to modify the network parameters.

The learning process will also have several internal variables that affect the learning process. These are called hyperparameters and while they have some influence on the learning process, they are not part of the network and not used during the inference stage.

Some training regimes have the potential to redefine the topology of the neural network. For example, in addition to modifying weights and biases, neurons can be removed ('pruned') from hidden layers (if, for example, the weights are all approaching zero for a specific neuron) thus dynamically modifying the network structure because a neuron having a near-zero weight value is unlikely to affect the output.

Datasets and generalization

To achieve good generalization, ANNs require large quantities of annotated training data. In the specific example of classification, these should ideally be balanced across categories (e.g. images of dogs, cats, horses and sheep) allowing the network to identify the features within the input data that are associated with each category. A phenomenon of overfitting occurs when the trained network does not generalize properly for unseen data. Underfitting means that the trained network has not sufficiently learnt the training data. It is a balance between under- and overfitting as controlled by the complexity of the network in terms of (a) the number of neurons per layer and (b) the overall number of layers between the input and output layers.

A pattern recognition machine

Once an ANN has been trained, we move to the second stage and use it to infer, in an exemplary and easy-to-understand case, classifications (predictions) with new data examples (previously unseen by the network during training). Here the network topology and the parameters remain frozen (static). This allows the specific implementation of this pattern recognition machine (inference engine) to be implemented in a range of ways and forms.

Although AI and ANNs are often discussed in the context of a software emulation, as I have mentioned above, that is not necessarily the case. Specialist hardware from companies like

NVIDIA and Graphcore provide hardware architectures that produce the topologies of ANNs, allowing a direct mapping of the network architecture to the hardware architecture. This approach makes running a trained ANN much quicker than via software simulation, especially given the ubiquitous availability of computers. This is becoming more important as the topology of ANNs becomes increasingly larger. Such hardware acceleration is also being extensively used to train ANNs, as this is a more computationally intensive process. Such hardware approaches are used both in research and in commercial projects.

In software emulations the same architecture is simulated (or emulated), operating in the same manner. Software and hardware implementations are the same in terms of the architecture, weights and biases, and the outputs produced. It is just a question of which is more convenient or efficient to use in any particular scenario.

Learning approaches

There are four main types of machine learning: supervised learning, unsupervised learning, semi-supervised learning and reinforcement learning:

1 In **supervised learning**, the algorithm is trained on a labelled dataset, where the correct output is provided for each example. This type of learning is used for tasks like regression and classification.
2 In **unsupervised learning**, the algorithm is not provided with labelled examples, and must discover the underlying structure of the data through techniques like clustering and dimensionality reduction.
3 In **semi-supervised learning**, the algorithm is provided with a partially labelled dataset, and must learn from both the labelled and unlabelled examples.

4 In **reinforcement learning**, the algorithm learns by interacting with its environment and receiving rewards or penalties for certain actions.

Machine learning has a wide range of applications, including image and speech recognition, natural language processing and predictive analytics. What we have seen over the last few years is an explosion of applications using machine learning, delivering a wide range of new functional capabilities across many different industries (from financial services to manufacturing and healthcare) and within all parts of the business operations (front-office, back-office, customer service and supply chain logistics to name a few).

Supervised learning

In supervised learning, the goal is to train a model to make predictions based on labelled examples. There are two main types of supervised learning: regression and classification.

Regression involves predicting a continuous output value, such as a price or a probability. Common algorithms for regression include linear regression, logistic regression and support vector machines.

Classification involves predicting a discrete output value, such as a label or a class. Common algorithms for classification include k-nearest neighbours, decision trees and naive Bayes.

Evaluating the performance of a supervised learning model is important to ensure that it is making accurate predictions. Common evaluation metrics for regression include mean squared error and mean absolute error, while common evaluation metrics for classification include accuracy, precision and recall.

Overfitting and underfitting are common issues that can arise when training a supervised learning model. Overfitting occurs when the model is too complex and is able to fit the training data perfectly but generalizes poorly to new data. Underfitting occurs when the model is too simple and is unable to capture the underlying pattern of the data.

Unsupervised learning

In unsupervised learning, the goal is to discover the underlying structure of the data without any prior knowledge or labels. There are three main types of unsupervised learning: clustering, dimensionality reduction and anomaly detection.

Clustering involves grouping similar data points together into clusters. Common algorithms for clustering include k-means, hierarchical clustering and density-based spatial clustering of applications with noise.

Dimensionality reduction involves reducing the number of dimensions in a dataset while retaining as much information as possible. This can be useful for visualizing high-dimensional data or for reducing the computational cost of training a model. Common algorithms for dimensionality reduction include principal component analysis and singular value decomposition.

Anomaly detection involves identifying data points that are unusual or do not conform to the expected pattern. This can be useful for detecting fraud, errors or unusual behaviour.

Semi-supervised learning

Semi-supervised learning is a type of machine learning that falls between supervised and unsupervised learning. In semi-supervised learning, the algorithm is provided with a partially labelled dataset, and must learn from both the labelled and unlabelled examples.

Semi-supervised learning can be useful in situations where it is costly or time-consuming to label a large dataset, but a small amount of labelled data is still available. It can also be used to improve the performance of a supervised learning model by providing additional training examples.

Some common algorithms for semi-supervised learning include support vector machines, self-training and co-training.

Reinforcement learning

Reinforcement learning is a type of machine learning in which an agent learns by interacting with its environment and receiving rewards or penalties for certain actions. The goal is for the agent to learn a policy that maximizes the cumulative reward over time.

Reinforcement learning has a wide range of applications, including robotics, control systems and games. It has been used to develop successful artificial intelligence systems for tasks like playing chess and Go.

There are three main types of reinforcement learning: value-based, policy-based and model-based.

Final thoughts

Machine learning (defining a predictive model from data) is the largest and most successful subfield of AI to date. It really breaks the mould of how we have traditionally built technology. Previously, decision logic and algorithms were functionally defined by business analysts working with business users who understood how they wanted the applications that supported their work to function.

This major modification of how complex algorithms (or in ML terms, models) are created is transformational within the IT sector, and for those unfamiliar with how ML works, it can initially be difficult to adjust to. It is not just this change in how algorithms are defined, it's the uncertainty of the data science practice with the need for experimentation of both the data and the types of ML used to gain best performance.

Innovation and research within machine learning is the driving force behind all the recent successes we have seen (with thousands of ML papers published each month). The investment in applied research in many of the largest tech firms is moving

ML forward at an incredible rate, and there is huge potential for further innovation in this space over the next decade and beyond.

While the focus has been on building machines that can learn, we really need a full range of intelligence abilities, including understanding, reasoning, knowledge representation, emotional awareness and common sense amongst others to move us towards human levels of intelligence.

In this chapter we have covered a broad range of ML techniques and methodologies to give anyone new to the topic a solid foundational understanding of what machine learning is all about and the core concepts involved.

We have concentrated on the main area of machine learning, neural networks, which is inspired by the neurons within biological brains, as this has been the most successful technique with the advances of deep learning methodologies in recent years.

In many ways, machine learning is the foundation on which AI applications and systems are built. While ML covers a wide range of techniques, there are many other approaches outside of ML that still sit within the broader field of AI. Often solutions will require a combination of technologies that span across both ML and AI.

CHAPTER SEVEN

Data and infrastructure

Data is the fuel that powers AI and ML; without it nothing is possible. In fact, the technologies such as big data platforms and cloud computing have been key enablers of the achievements of AI over the last decade or so. We have been storing and analysing much more data in the last few years than we have in the previous decade; each year the amount of data that is saved is increasing at an unprecedented rate. Actually, we have so much data that it is becoming a challenge to both store it and analyse it.

One of the core activities for data scientists is the organization and pre-processing of the data needed to both train and test ML models. In many cases, this can become a significant part of the overall process of building ML models, as it often requires experimentation in terms of the dataset used and the features exposed within the available data fields.

The data management systems and data processing tools available to data scientists can make a huge difference in the speed and performance of the work done and the resulting quality of ML models.

In this chapter we will highlight the various considerations, platforms, frameworks and tools available to data science teams to collect and pre-process the data needed to build the predictive models needed. We also highlight some of the challenges and the latest technology advances available in data infrastructure and management.

Data foundations

Data plays a vital role in the field of AI and machine learning. Data scientists who build ML models will spend approximately 80 per cent of their time working with the data used to train and test a model. This includes selection of the right set of data, data cleansing, feature selection, data bias removal, data quality improvements, data labelling and even, when required, synthetic data creation.

Data management has evolved over many decades, from transactional databases to data warehouses, big data stores, data lakes, data fabrics and now the data mesh, but all are aimed at bringing enterprise data together and allowing different data consumers the capabilities to interact with the data in the ways they need.

The task of data science can be greatly improved with easy access to data in one place with the tools to manipulate and transform data, referred to as data pre-processing.

We also acknowledge that the data strategy and foundations are constantly changing as part of ongoing programmes of work to upgrade the data management, consolidate infrastructure, migrate to the cloud and leverage the latest architectural designs and technologies.

Modern data platforms and architecture

Since the 1990s and early 2000s, with the introduction of big data technologies allowing data to be consolidated from multiple sources to enable more computationally intensive analytics and reporting, the area of data management and data infrastructure has rapidly evolved. This was amplified with the introduction of cloud computing in 2006 by AWS (Amazon with its Elastic Compute EC2 service). Since then, we have seen the evolution of data infrastructures continue to innovate with data lakes (2011) and data mesh (2019).

360 customer view

Often, through the long-term development of systems and applications, client or customer data becomes scattered across the organization, mastered in different data repositories, and without the implementation of a data mesh, providing access to the right data to the right people can be challenging.

Best practice now looks to develop a 360 view of customer data, allowing a complete picture of a customer which will then better inform decision-making and analytics across the applications and functions of the business.

FIGURE 7.1   Data layers with analytics, AI and automation

FIGURE 7.2   360 customer view

Data pre-processing pipelines

To prepare training and testing data for ML models and to do the same transformations as part of the model inference, a data pipeline will need to be created to shape the data into the correct format for the machine learning models.

These data pipelines will sit on top of the data layer within the enterprise architecture; they can operate in various modes, from real-time streaming to batch-based, and form a critical component of the overall tech stack for AI/ML implementations.

Structured and unstructured data

Most businesses, regardless of industry, will have a mix of structured and unstructured data. Leveraging unstructured data in ways that surface valuable information and insights is a key element of any modern data management and processing platform. The introduction of big data technologies, NoSQL query languages and flexible data schemas opened up possibilities to use data from documents and other sources that would have

FIGURE 7.3   Data as a service capabilities

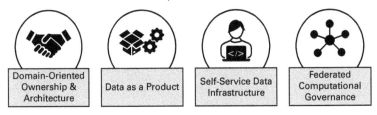

Domain-Oriented Ownership & Architecture	Data as a Product	Self-Service Data Infrastructure	Federated Computational Governance

been more challenging with transactional relational databases. There are approaches and architectures that can support the analysis and processing of unstructured data.

Data as a service (DaaS)

With modern data architectures, the approach is to consider data as a service, allowing producers and consumers to be more in control of the data they own or need. Figure 7.3 illustrates some of the core considerations for this data-centric focus.

Data governance and data lineage

With the considerable importance of data to machine learning, having strong audit, governance and traceability (data lineage) is a major requirement for both the data science team and the IT management, providing audit and transparency in model development.

There are various tools and frameworks available that can be used to provide data lineage and audit of data used with the training of different ML models. This will help give full transparency and governance of the models in production and the data used to train and test them. This also helps the data science teams when they need to update models in the future. The need for this type of capability will rise as the volume of models deployed increases.

Technical infrastructure and architecture

There are two aspects to the technical infrastructure from an AI and machine learning perspective. The first relates to the overall process and workflow of developing an ML model, which requires most of the heavy lifting (if any bespoke or refinement training is needed) and the second is the inference of the model (that is, using the trained model in a live or production environment). Depending on the size of the ML model used, even inference can be relatively computationally expensive (the largest generative AI models or large language models still require a GPU to run the model).

The impact on the technical infrastructure also depends on the delivery approach. If using a vendor or consultant, the technical complexity of training the model might be shared or fully outsourced. If using a model pre-trained by a cloud provider, the focus would be on integrating API calls to that model from other parts of the software application.

There will also be situations when third-party ML models are used and exposed via a simple API call, and therefore the use and integration is at the application layer to ensure the right models are called from the correct technical environments. There may be a need for load balancing and call throttling to properly control the use of such services.

Cloud platforms

The cloud providers have many in-house ML models that can be used as part of an AI solution. For many standard capabilities, all will have similar models that perform to comparable levels. However, there will be more advanced functional requirements that one cloud provider has that others don't, or one performs significantly better than others. In these situations, we will need to be more purposeful in the architectural design and implementation to ensure we are delivering the best results for clients regardless of their preferred cloud platform.

For internal processes and productivity enhancements, these considerations will be less restrictive, allowing us more freedom to select the best options.

Scalable architecture

For both training and inference, the key is designing a scalable architecture that allows capacity growth with user consumption. Here the cloud platforms come into their own and provide blueprint architectures that enable dynamic (or otherwise) horizontal scalability to keep the systems performing at appropriate levels.

The data science workflow and process

A key new set of requirements as one introduces data science and machine learning into the mix of technical delivery will be the data science workflow and development process for data science. I will cover this in detail in the next section but it's worth acknowledging here that there is a need to ensure a fit between the current technology footprint and any new tools and frameworks introduced for data science.

The specific needs of the data science team will evolve over time, as the team matures and as the scale of AI and ML delivery increases. Each team and lead of data science will also have their own preference toolset.

One of the biggest risks to AI/ML deployment is the alignment between the current technology footprint and the additions needed for data science deployments. Often the data science team will have a multitude of tools they use during the prototyping and development and only worry about the production environment towards the end of the first delivery. This can cause unnecessary delays and potential conflicts that may be challenging to resolve.

Care is needed to map out requirements across all technology environments so a smooth transition into live production is possible.

MLOps

Machine learning operations (or MLOps) is an extension of the function of DevOps but specific to the nuances of developing machine learning models. For large-scale data science teams, tools and frameworks to facilitate automation around the operations of building, deploying and testing machine learning will become essential.

The specific MLOps tools used will be a function of the preferences of the data science team members, the other data science tools being used and the scale of work being done. The MLOps functions would normally be built and managed by an ML engineer, but in smaller teams one of the data scientists could look to perform this role too.

Sometimes the term AIOps is also used for this function but it can also be used, confusingly, to refer to AI applied to the operations area more generally.

Training vs inference

There are two distinct activities when building machine learning models and they have different data and computational requirements, which alters the architecture needed to support each.

For training, a fundamental requirement is to manipulate datasets, pre-processing data to improve data quality, data cleansing, data transformation and data reduction to produce a set of signals that can be used to train the model. Training a model is computationally intensive, as the topology and hyperparameters need to be optimized via trial and error to maximize the performance of the trained model.

Once a model is trained, the use of the model (known as inference) has a different data and computational profile, still needing similar data pre-processing, but the computational setup needs to be focused on scaled running of the model on an ad hoc basis aligned to user demand.

Typically, the technical architectures for training and inference are different, but need to be aligned to allow smooth progress from the development of models to deployment into a production environment.

Trained models are usually exposed to the rest of the IT infrastructure and applications via an API, calls to the API will activate the model by presenting it with a set of input signals, and the model will provide the related output response that is then passed back via the API to the calling application.

Monitoring performance

There will be a need to monitor the running and performance of deployed models. This is because model performance can degrade over time, as the data can shift or drift over a period of time (as users change the way they work and how they use the systems and data). This can be dealt with by retraining the model with more up-to-date information; for example, you might retrain a model once a month to include the last month's data so that it captures the most recent information.

Deploying a model into production is only part of the pipeline process (not the end, as it might be with other IT systems); continued monitoring and performance testing with potential retraining are potential needs for many models.

Infrastructure and platform options

All of the cloud providers – Amazon, Microsoft, Google, IBM, Alibaba, Oracle and Salesforce – have frameworks, tools and pre-trained models available to clients and integrated into applications and solutions. They provide the major building blocks but there still needs to be substantial effort to turn them into proper AI/ML capabilities that data science teams are comfortable to use as part of their process and workflow.

There are also specialist platforms from vendors; two of the most well-known are from H20 and C3. They have a range of scalable platforms for enterprise users looking to deploy AI at scale.

Home-grown platforms

Some organizations, and we have seen this extensively in the financial services sector, prefer to build their own bespoke platforms, pulling together a collection of tools and frameworks from various sources.

This option gives the most flexibility and control but would cost the most to establish and maintain. This option would only really make sense if you had a significantly large volume of data to process (financial services can have millions of transactions per hour) and needed to make rapid and frequent changes to the system.

Organizations will increasingly see the ML models they use being the crown jewels in terms of the algorithmic capabilities of the firm, the underlying platforms becoming more commoditized, as we have seen with the big data and cloud technologies. Therefore it is a firm's unique datasets and the ability to develop bespoke ML models that will create the competitive advantage with AI implementations.

Final thoughts

In this chapter we have explored how important data is for the delivery of AI and ML functionality, but also how challenging and complicated it can be. The best-in-class data scientists need the best possible data management and infrastructure to make it easier to select training and testing datasets to produce the most performant models. This chapter also provides a range of suggested frameworks and tools that can help construct a best-in-class data processing workflow.

Being able to extract the greatest number of insights from the underlying data available within any organization is going to be a core requirement for businesses to make better decisions and understand their customers to provide a more personalized service.

Moving towards more real-time reporting and dashboards is also a key improvement to enable more reactive decision making which can help organizations deal with dynamic environmental and economic changes more quickly than would otherwise be possible.

However, to deliver this level of digital transformation requires some level of investment (and time) depending on where your data infrastructure is currently.

Data management is an evolving subject that will need to improve in certain areas to support the specific needs of AI in the coming years. This goes beyond data lineage and audit, to the ability to support rigorous data privacy methodologies that work for both data owners and data users.

With AI safety and digital trust becoming hot topics, the data infrastructure layers will need to innovate to accommodate such requirements to future-proof themselves and help deliver more advanced analytics requirements.

CHAPTER EIGHT

Advanced topics

This chapter covers a range of more specialized and in-depth topics in data science, such as deep learning, natural language processing, big data, distributed computing and quantum computing.

Deep learning

Deep learning is a type of machine learning that uses artificial neural networks with many layers of neurons, various network architectures and different learning algorithms. It has achieved state-of-the-art results in tasks like image and speech recognition, natural language processing and machine translation.

The success of deep learning was the catalyst that has rejuvenated the AI industry over the last 10 years or so. However, deep learning requires large amounts of data and computational power, and it is often used in conjunction with techniques like transfer learning and fine-tuning to achieve good performance.

Many of the recent advances in AI are due to the capabilities of deep learning and as a data scientist you will most likely use and develop many deep learning models.

Natural language

Natural language processing (NLP) is a subfield of artificial intelligence that deals with the interaction between computers and human language. It involves pre-processing and interpreting text data, and can be used for tasks like text classification, sentiment analysis and machine translation.

There are other areas of natural language AI including natural language generation (NLG), which is primarily focused on the creation of text (and sits within the generative AI field too), and natural language understanding (NLU), which is more involved with how we can make machines actually properly understand language.

For NLP, there are various stages of the process, including pre-processing and feature extraction.

Pre-processing text data typically involves cleaning and normalizing the text and converting it into a numerical representation that can be used as input to a machine learning model. This can involve techniques like stemming, lemmatization and stop word removal.

Feature extraction and representation involves extracting relevant information and patterns from the text data, and representing them in a way that can be used by a machine learning model. This can involve techniques like bag of words, term frequency-inverse document frequency (TF-IDF) and word embeddings.

Video and image analytics

Video analytics is the process of analysing video data to extract insights and information. It can be used for a wide range of applications such as surveillance, traffic management and customer behaviour analysis.

Machine learning plays a key role in video analytics, as it enables the development of algorithms that can automatically learn and improve over time. By using machine learning, video analytics systems can learn to recognize patterns and features in the video data and can make predictions or decisions based on this information.

Some common machine learning techniques that are used in video analytics include object recognition, facial recognition and activity recognition. These techniques can be used to identify and classify objects, people and events in the video data, and to extract relevant information and insights.

Video analytics systems can also be used in combination with other technologies, such as sensor networks and IoT devices, to enable a wide range of applications and scenarios. For example, a video analytics system could be used to monitor traffic patterns and alert authorities to potential accidents or congestion, or to analyse customer behaviour in a retail store and provide insights for improving the shopping experience.

We must note that applications of facial recognition have been deemed highly controversial by many in the industry and wider society. As a result, some technology firms have stopped building capability in this particular application area.

Generative algorithms

Generative algorithms are a class of machine learning algorithms that are designed to generate new data samples that are similar to a training dataset. These algorithms are trained on a dataset and then can generate new samples that are similar to the training data.

Generative algorithms have a wide range of applications in various fields. Some examples of the applications of generative algorithms include:

Image generation: Generative algorithms can be used to generate new images that are similar to a training dataset of images. For example, a generative adversarial network (GAN) can be trained on a dataset of images of faces, and then can generate new, synthetic images of faces that are similar to the training data.

Natural language processing: Generative algorithms can be used to generate text that is similar to a training dataset of text. For example, a generative algorithm can be trained on a dataset of movie reviews, and then can generate new, synthetic reviews that are similar to the training data.

Speech synthesis: Generative algorithms can be used to generate synthetic speech that is similar to a training dataset of speech. For example, a generative algorithm can be trained on a dataset of human speech, and then can generate new, synthetic speech that is similar to the training data.

Music generation: Generative algorithms can be used to generate new music that is similar to a training dataset of music. For example, a generative algorithm can be trained on a dataset of music tracks, and then can generate new, synthetic music tracks that are similar to the training data.

Some examples of generative algorithms include:

GANs: GANs are a type of neural network that consists of two networks: a generator network and a discriminator network. The generator network is trained to generate new samples that are similar to the training data, and the discriminator network is trained to distinguish between real and fake samples.

Variational Autoencoders (VAEs): VAEs are a type of neural network that consists of an encoder and a decoder. The encoder is trained to compress the input data into a lower-dimensional representation, and the decoder is trained to reconstruct the input data from the lower-dimensional representation. VAEs can be used to generate new samples by sampling from the latent space and passing them through the decoder.

Restricted Boltzmann Machines (RBMs): RBMs are a type of generative model that consists of two layers of interconnected nodes: a visible layer and a hidden layer. RBMs can be trained to reconstruct the input data, and they can also be used to generate new samples by sampling from the hidden layer.

The world of generative AI

Generative AI has changed the face of AI and machine learning, and with so many tools commonly available, it is now easier than ever before for people to try the capabilities.

Many people are seeing how generative AI can be used to improve individual productivity, using the foundational LLMs to accelerate the creative process for all sorts of documents and materials needed across many different roles, from sales and marketing to technology, business development and customer support, to name a few.

However, while the generic foundational models are proving to be very useful and capable, many companies are realizing they need a more bespoke custom model to perform well for their specific use-case, potentially using their own corporate data to add context to prompts and thus producing more accurate results.

Leveraging knowledge bases and technologies like knowledge graphs to provide the contextual information via co-pilot orchestration is showing the way in providing more tailored and customized text generation that delivers real value for specific use-cases.

Generative AI isn't just about text; we are seeing major inroads being made on image and video generation and manipulation too.

Music is also undergoing disruption from generative AI tools that will shape the way music is used in many areas, including for digital assistants and the metaverse.

More advanced uses of generative AI include invention and design; here it is still very early days, but this area will advance rapidly over the next few years.

Prompt engineering

In 2022, with the introduction of various generative and conversational AI foundational models, a new role and skill became key for getting the most out of these new AI models. Referred to as prompt engineering, we have seen firms hiring people who have an aptitude for the creation of prompts that get the best results from these LLMs.

We also saw a flood of prompt cheat sheets for different topics, again focused on getting the best out of these foundational models. Foundational models can be used for many different things, from writing poetry to programming code, so knowing how to phrase the prompts is a key component to optimize the desired results.

However, we also know that for certain tasks, the foundational models need additional context, and this information may need to be added to supplement the specific prompt, again to help maximize the results from the model.

The data science toolbox

Data science notebooks

One of the key tools for data scientists is what is known as the data science notebook.

Data science notebooks are interactive documents that allow data scientists to combine code, text and visualizations in a single document. They are widely used in the field of data science for tasks such as data exploration, visualization and machine learning. This is akin to the integrated development environments (IDEs) used by other developers.

Some popular examples of data science notebooks include:

- **Jupyter Notebook:** Jupyter Notebook is an open-source web application that allows data scientists to create and share documents that contain live code, equations, visualizations and narrative text. Jupyter Notebook can be used with a number of different programming languages, including Python, R and Julia.
- **Google Colab:** Google Colab is a cloud-based data science notebook platform that allows data scientists to write and execute code, and to share and collaborate on notebooks with other users. Google Colab provides access to a range of tools and resources, including GPUs and TPUs for machine learning.
- **Azure Notebooks:** Azure Notebooks is a cloud-based data science notebook platform provided by Microsoft Azure. It allows data scientists to write and execute code, and to share and collaborate on notebooks with other users. Azure Notebooks provides access to a range of tools and resources, including machine learning libraries and data visualization tools.
- **Amazon SageMaker Studio:** An IDE that provides a single web-based visual interface where you can access purpose-built tools to perform all machine learning development steps, from preparing data to building, training and deploying your ML models.

Data science notebooks provide a convenient and interactive platform for data scientists to develop and share their work. They allow data scientists to easily combine code, text and visualizations in a single document, and to collaborate and share their work with others.

These notebooks also provide a way to record what was done during the experimental phase of building an ML model, as often there is a lot of trial and error, and it can get difficult to recall what was done if it is not audited properly.

Data science tools and frameworks

There is simply a multitude of data science tools available, many open source, and each data scientist will have preferences and experience with different tools. Typically, the data science team together (with guidance from the lead data scientist or head of data science) would define the preferred toolset to use.

For large organizations, this can be a problem when you have several separate data science teams, each defining their own set of tools. This is when a central hub or workgroup can help to standardize across teams/groups to make it easier to share between teams. Some examples of data science tools are:

- **TensorFlow:** An open-source library for machine learning and artificial intelligence, developed by Google. TensorFlow is designed to be flexible and scalable, and it is widely used for a range of tasks including image and speech recognition, natural language processing and machine translation.
- **PyTorch:** An open-source library for machine learning and artificial intelligence, developed by Meta. PyTorch is designed to be easy to use and flexible, and it is **widely used for tasks such as computer vision, natural language processing and deep learning.**
- **scikit-learn:** An open-source library for machine learning in Python. scikit-learn **provides a range of algorithms and tools for tasks such as classification, regression, clustering and dimensionality reduction.**
- **Keras:** An open-source library for deep learning in Python. Keras is designed to be easy to use and provides a high-level interface for building and training deep learning models.

- **MXNet:** An open-source library for deep learning. MXNet is designed to be fast and scalable, and it is widely used for tasks such as image and speech recognition, natural language processing and machine translation.
- **Theano:** An open-source library for numerical computation and machine learning in Python. Theano is designed to be efficient and flexible, and it is widely used for tasks such as deep learning and natural language processing.
- **Caffe:** An open-source library for deep learning, developed by the Berkeley Vision and Learning Center. Caffe is designed to be fast and efficient, and it is widely used for tasks such as image and speech recognition.

SPECIALIST TOOLS AND FRAMEWORKS

There are also many specialist tools and frameworks for different tasks, from video analytics to natural language processing, as well as tools to help with the data science workflow (also referred to as MLOps).

Here is a short list of NLP dedicated tools:

- **spaCy:** spaCy is an open-source NLP library that is designed for production-level **use. It provides fast and accurate tools for tokenization, part-of-speech tagging,** dependency parsing and named entity recognition, and is available in multiple languages.
- **NLTK:** The Natural Language Toolkit (NLTK) is a widely used NLP library that is written in Python. It provides a wide range of tools and resources for tasks such as tokenization, stemming and part-of-speech tagging, as well as tools for working with linguistic corpora and annotated text.
- **GPT-4:** GPT-4 (Generative Pre-trained Transformer 4) is a state-of-the-art NLP model developed by OpenAI. It is a transformer-based model that can perform a wide range of NLP tasks, including language translation, summarization and question answering.

- **BERT:** BERT (Bidirectional Encoder Representations from Transformers) is a transformer-based NLP model developed by Google. It is designed for tasks such as language understanding, sentiment analysis and natural language generation, and has achieved state-of-the-art results on a wide range of NLP benchmarks.
- **Flair:** Flair is an open-source NLP library that is built on top of PyTorch. It provides tools for tasks such as part-of-speech tagging, named entity recognition and text classification, and is designed to be easy to use and integrate into existing NLP pipelines.

For video and image analytics:

- **OpenCV:** OpenCV is an open-source computer vision library that provides tools for tasks such as object detection, face recognition and motion analysis. It can be used to build custom video analytics applications or to integrate video analytics capabilities into existing systems.
- **DeepVision:** DeepVision is a video analytics platform developed by DeepVision AI. It provides tools for tasks such as object detection, facial recognition and event detection, and can be used to build custom video analytics applications or to integrate video analytics capabilities into existing systems.
- **Amazon Rekognition:** Amazon Rekognition is a cloud-based video analytics platform developed by Amazon Web Services. It provides tools for tasks such as object detection, facial recognition and scene analysis, and can be used to build custom video analytics applications or to integrate video analytics capabilities into existing systems.
- **Google Cloud Video Intelligence:** Google Cloud Video Intelligence is a cloud-based video analytics platform developed by Google. It provides tools for tasks such as object detection, facial recognition and scene analysis, and can be used to build custom video analytics applications or to integrate video analytics capabilities into existing systems.

Distributed computing

Distributed computing and specifically, with an AI lens, federated learning, has a number of interesting applications where data needs to be kept secure, but the insights from training an ML model can be shared and aggregated to deliver a better combined model.

An example of this might be when various banks want to pool knowledge to build a federated model for fraud detection, but do not want to share the underlying data with their competitors. However, all contributing entities are keen to benefit from an aggregated (or combined) model that would be better at detecting fraudulent activity than any one individual model from a single bank.

Federated learning can be implemented at the enterprise level, as described in the previous example, or can be used in a more consumer type of application; however, this is more challenging as the number of models to aggregate increases with the number of end-users.

This is interesting because an increasing focus on data privacy and data trust, federated learning and more generally distributed computing provides the approach that puts data privacy front and centre.

Quantum computing

The potential of quantum computing, when it becomes commercially scaled, will significantly impact the way machine learning, and specifically deep learning, is built. It will reduce the training time to the point that building the largest of LLMs will become dramatically faster, being able to try many different datasets, architectures and parameterizations.

This will not only accelerate the advancement of the most cutting-edge AI algorithms and the resulting models, but it could disrupt the cloud and hardware providers.

Quantum computing will also open the door to solving the most complex problems that were previously unachievable. Many believe this will also accelerate us towards the moonshot of AGI.

When will this happen? Probably sooner than we might assume – potentially before 2030. When it does arrive, it will change the world in so many different ways.

Data privacy and trust

There are several aspects of data privacy that need to be considered with respect to AI.

The first, and arguably the most controversial, is related to the use of data for training of large foundational models. The big tech firms have crawled the internet and pulled every bit of information they can find to use as training data. While this data is technically in the public domain, we have not given permission for our own information to be included in these models. No doubt opinion will be divided on this. Some people will be okay and comfortable with their data being used and happy for that to have been done without express permission. Some will be happy for their information to be used but would have welcomed the invitation and the ability to opt out, while others would have wanted to immediately opt out of this scheme. Obviously, there is huge benefit in leveraging mass quantities of information from a diverse range of contributors, and the task of asking everyone's permission might have been practically unfeasible. However, there is a real move towards providing the option for people to request that their data be removed (or unlearnt) from such models. Ultimately, we need to build the infrastructures that allow data protection and trust to be built into the ways data is collected, managed and used.

There are other issues, such as training data being exposed with the use of a trained neural network; this type of attack has been easily demonstrated and could be used to reverse-engineer private information about an individual that they wouldn't want exposed publicly.

Data trust is an area that also spans many topics, but the key here is to build trust as a data steward that the appropriate permissions and controls are in place between the data owner and the data user. Data trust covers aspects of data privacy and protection, but also more ethical concerns that data is used appropriately and for purposes that the data owners would be supportive of. Data trust is also built with transparency of decision making by algorithms, so that people can better understand why a particular result is produced if they want to challenge it.

Intellectual property rights

Machine learning algorithms often rely on large amounts of data to learn and improve. However, this data may contain sensitive or personal information about individuals, which can raise concerns about data privacy. There is a risk that this data could be accessed or used in ways that violate privacy laws or individuals' rights.

Machine learning algorithms can be used to create new products, services and insights, which can raise questions about who owns the intellectual property rights to these creations. There may be disputes about whether the creators of the algorithms or the owners of the data used to train them have the rights to the resulting creations.

The concerns around data privacy and IP rights are still to be worked out; the challenge is that these topics are not easy to resolve, with complexity on both sides of the argument. As the technology matures it is likely that capabilities will be built in to give these issues more consideration.

Regulation

The regulatory landscape for AI is changing just as rapidly as the technology itself, with several countries now publishing AI laws to govern the use of primarily foundational models to protect citizens. We see countries taking very different stances on AI regulation, some with a more aggressive perspective and others more supportive of AI innovation.

A new era of computing – generative waves

Welcome to the start of the new era of computing, an era of creative computing or generative computing.

While it might seem that generative AI only started in 2022 with ChatGPT, there have been elements of generative computing for many years.

To help understand how generative computing has developed I have grouped the different advances into waves, each more advanced and capable than the previous one. And each wave is arriving faster than the last.

The first wave – code writing code (algorithms)

A major technological advancement was when you could write programs that create and compile new programs. This can sound somewhat counterintuitive to anyone outside of the technology field but being able to algorithmically generate new code and algorithms is a major step.

Personally, I first saw this with the C# language, but I am sure this is now possible with many others. While this capability had been available for many years, its potential had not really been understood or realized.

While this ability was technically possible, it was not adopted widely; however, with the latest generative AI we see a strong utility of code-generation support programmers with co-pilots integrated into development environments to support and accelerate the process of writing code.

The second wave – data (and learning algorithms) writing predictive algorithms (models)

Taking historical data to define the algorithm of the trained predictive model is essentially another form of using one algorithm to create another. However, using data directly to define an algorithm was a quantum leap and has opened up a world of possibilities that has driven the advances we have seen over the last decade or so.

This major sub-field of AI, known as machine learning, has been the most successful area of AI over the last 20 years or so. We have shown that such training algorithms can extract information and rules from large datasets in a way that humans would struggle to do. This moved us away from building expert systems with predefined logic and rules to these data-driven predictive models.

We are seeing applications of this type of approach across all industry sectors and new start-ups are being launched every day to exploit new datasets.

The third wave – algorithms creating content

This then evolved into what we now call generative algorithms.

Where the second wave was simply producing predictive outputs, with this third wave the output is more detailed and complex – and represents a transformation of its input. The technology for this was grounded in the application of language translation, converting one language to another.

While the technology continued to focus on text generation, we also saw initial versions taking images and changing the style of the artwork, or taking one image and outputting variations of it based on simple factors. Here the input is an image to manipulate or use as the basis for the transformation to generate the output.

These generative algorithms have been improving over the last few years, allowing more accurate transformations and manipulations of input content. No doubt you will have seen various demos of this type of technique, from paintings being animated, to fake videos of actors and politicians.

The advances in generative AI over the last few years have been astonishing.

The fourth wave – algorithms creating content via prompts

We are now seeing with various advanced ML generative models the ability to generate both images and now videos from text-based prompting. This prompting is essentially guiding the algorithm in its generation.

This is a step change from the previous wave, based on the type of input used. Now termed as prompting, we can provide a text-based request or query that is used to generate the output (text, image, video or music).

We have seen advances here where the prompting has moved to more conversational interactions, allowing users to respond back to first attempts at generation to make changes and enhancements to refine the second response.

The technology in this wave has been developing at speed, with the introduction of co-pilots to orchestrate the augmentation of prompts with additional context to help make the output responses even more specific and accurate.

The fifth wave – algorithms creating anything via prompts

Many experts believe that recent advancements can only improve with additional human intervention and oversight. What this really means is that the technology lacks any form of understanding and until it does, its capabilities will be limited and potentially constrain how the technology may be used in real-world practical applications.

The fifth wave will be a true fusion of human and artificial intelligence, where we simply have to ask for something to be created and within seconds we have what we need, from new computer programs to perform specific tasks, to generative algorithms that can produce new films or music in a style we like with the storyline we specify.

This will evolve into digital assistants that are able to do our bidding on many different tasks we request.

The impact of this level of generative computing on different industries is yet to be determined, but it is likely to dramatically change business models over the next few years. Companies and individuals will need to determine how they can adapt to this new wave of technology that is evolving so fast. The real challenge is being able to keep up with the rate of advancement and to be able to take these new technologies and embed them into existing businesses in a way that adds benefits and avoids detrimental impacts.

The sixth wave – algorithms inventing and innovating

The natural extension of the fifth wave is to have AI able to create new inventions and innovations that humans have not yet devised, using advanced understanding of several subjects and fusing them together.

What if we ask the computer to invent a new product? Or conduct research that uncovers new insights?

This of course opens huge legal and ethical questions – from copyright ownership to data privacy. In addition to the technical challenges to make this capability more robust, the fifth wave will need to address and solve many of these ethical questions before the technology is accepted widely.

The seventh wave – algorithms as autonomous entities

This may then lead to a seventh wave of algorithms acting as autonomous entities, able to make decisions and reason for themselves. Once we give an algorithm a task to achieve, it would automatically go off and work towards that goal, without any additional input from humans.

Termed as auto-pilots or digital assistants, these will soon become very capable in terms of performing tasks and fully automating complex actions.

Many people worry about this level of autonomous AI, as the goals must be aligned with humans and it would need to have common sense and the ability to question itself and ask for clarifications if it thinks something doesn't add up or make sense.

Final thoughts

In this chapter we have explored some of the advanced topics related to the field of AI. We have to acknowledge the speed of progress and the rate of change happening at the moment, which makes writing this chapter particularly challenging.

What is easy to predict is that we will see much more advanced topics for AI coming to light over the next few years, with more advanced approaches, algorithms, hardware, frameworks, tools and platforms moving us towards the moonshot goal of artificial general intelligence.

PART THREE

The process

Understanding the technology behind AI is only part of the battle. Building AI requires specific processes, workflows and a defined pipeline of checkpoints and tollgates to ensure the best-in-class models are deployed that meet all requirements including ethical, legal and regulatory considerations. Implementing and deploying the first AI use-case is also a world apart from a scaled approach to build and maintain tens if not hundreds of different ML models across the organization, especially if you have different data science teams looking after the various vertical departments.

There are also some potential pitfalls to the collaboration between data science teams and the rest of the IT organization. Different methodologies and approaches make alignment sometimes tough but not unsurmountable with understanding and a collaborative attitude.

The AI industry may have guidelines and best practices, but most companies and teams will define the details of how they wish to work, with each team and each company having slightly different approaches, workflows, processes, standards and policies.

As the technology advances, the maturity and professional approach will evolve, making the processes used much better, becoming well defined and standardized across teams, firms, industries and countries.

The technology, while advancing fast, is still very much in its infancy, and requires a professional approach to its design, construction, deployment and monitoring that is seen in other industries and professions. We need to learn fast and adopt best practice from other areas to minimize the risks of poor delivery.

CHAPTER NINE

Elements of an AI strategy

So let's start at the beginning. We are now seeing widespread adoption of AI across all sizes of businesses, from innovative start-ups to large corporations. The benefits of productivity gains alone are difficult for any business to ignore. This is also happening across most industries, including those that have until recently been technology laggards, resisting the adoption of any technical application or solution.

We can draw parallels with the adoption of the internet and companies building their own websites. Adoption was slow initially, but once the benefits of having a website became obvious, then the majority of businesses followed. With ChatGPT and other generative AI models and capabilities, the benefits of productivity improvements are now clearly obvious to the senior management of businesses large and small.

The desire and drive for AI adoption is now ever present, but the challenge is now finding the talent, knowledge and experience to adopt the technology. Many firms will have limited internal capability, and while it may be easy to start small and

FIGURE 9.1   The nine elements of an AI strategy

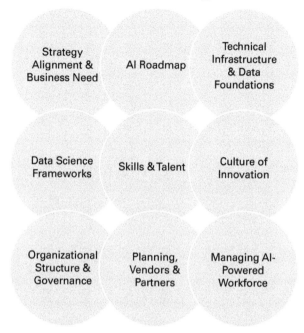

experiment with some of the off-the-shelf applications, doing anything more complex and bespoke can be more difficult without the right people, partners and support.

Consideration of the AI strategy by all employees working with or using AI within a company is important; having sight of the culture, ethics, policies, process and procedure around the use and adoption of AI is a clear advantage to the speed and responsible use of the technology.

This chapter will give insight into the consideration senior management and the board will be giving to the approach to AI adoption. Any significant transformation is a highly complex, time- and resource-consuming distraction that must be integrated with other programmes of work already scheduled and prioritized.

The nine elements of an AI strategy

These nine elements cover the significant aspects of an AI strategy, from identifying a business need to plans and priorities for AI implementation. It also details not just the technology, but the people, process, culture and governance as elements of an AI strategy.

Understanding the importance of each element of your own AI strategy will help accelerate the adoption of AI at scale and help avoid many of the potential pitfalls and challenges along the way.

One: Strategy alignment and business need

Businesses looking to start the journey of AI adoption will want to ensure there is alignment between the business and technology strategies and their roadmaps. Fundamentally, this is born from identifying the real business need for AI solutions. To do this the best approach is to start from the problem or challenge and work backwards, with the aim to identify correct solutions. Many of those potential problems could involve the use of AI and machine learning as part of the overall approach to deliver a solution.

Identifying a business need(s) for AI is always the starting point with any major initiative to implement AI within a company. It is easy to follow the hype and feel the pressure to adopt AI because everyone else appears to be using it. But AI, like any other technology, is a tool, a tool to help solve problems. The business drivers for AI need to be surfaced in solving real business problems and delivering value to the business and its customers.

Business value framework – return on investment

There are several different methods for assessing the business value of AI implementations and the return on investment (ROI).

For some use-cases the ROI will be clear and well understood, for others it may require more detailed analysis to determine the priority and appropriate approach.

Unquestionably, there are other tacit benefits and value to the organization from the adoption of AI, and we should also look at this from a portfolio perspective as well as individual use-cases.

It is essential for the overall success of AI adoption that the ROI for each project undertaken is well defined and measured afterwards to highlight the realized benefits of deployment.

Strategic alignment

Ensuring a strategic alignment between business objectives (business strategy) and technology strategy remains paramount for the successful execution of IT projects and programmes. Without this alignment, technology implementations are at risk of falling short in delivering the tangible value that business users require, potentially leading to project failures and wasted investments.

Amidst the AI hype, organizations may be tempted to adopt AI simply to keep pace with the trend, often without a clear understanding of where the true value lies or an assessment of the ROI.

Augmenting any IT strategy with a well-defined AI strategy becomes imperative to optimize outcomes in the adoption of AI within the organization. This approach enables the comprehensive evaluation of initial AI projects and offers substantial support for subsequent implementation cases.

Moreover, strategic alignment facilitates the adoption of a portfolio approach to AI adoption, particularly when dealing with numerous use-cases spanning various functions of the business.

Two: AI roadmap

One common mistake often observed when companies embark on their journey of adopting AI is their failure to implement an innovation funnel workflow. The decision to focus solely on one initial AI use-case can pose a substantial risk to the overall momentum of any AI programme, especially if that initial use-case does not successfully transition into a production environment, which can occur for various reasons, particularly since it's the first attempt.

A more prudent long-term strategy for organizations is to adopt a portfolio approach, simultaneously pursuing multiple AI projects, even distributing them across different segments of the company and teams. As long as these teams or groups collaborate and exchange insights, it can accelerate the adoption process and mitigate the risk of losing momentum if the initial project falls short of expectations.

Larger businesses usually have the advantage of having multiple departments and groups interested in initiating AI adoption, making this less of an issue. However, for smaller firms with limited resources, this constraint can pose a significant challenge and a risk to their AI adoption success.

Three: Technical infrastructure and data foundations

Technical infrastructure

When considering the technical infrastructure for AI and machine learning, it can be divided into two main areas. The first pertains to the comprehensive process and workflow involved in developing an ML model, which typically entails most of the heavy lifting, especially if custom tailoring or fine-tuning is required. The second aspect concerns the utilization of the trained model, known as inference, within a live or production environment. It's worth noting that even the inference stage can incur significant computational costs, especially when dealing with large ML models, such as the most expansive generative AI models or sizable language models, which often necessitate the use of GPUs for smooth execution.

The impact on the technical infrastructure is also contingent upon the chosen delivery approach. If an organization opts for a vendor or consultant, the technical complexity of model training may be shared or entirely outsourced. Alternatively, if a pre-trained model from a cloud provider is employed, the focus shifts towards seamlessly integrating API calls to that model from various parts of the software application.

In certain instances, third-party ML models may be utilized and made accessible through straightforward API calls. Consequently, the utilization and integration primarily occur at the application layer to ensure that the appropriate models are invoked within the correct technical environments. In such scenarios, there might be a necessity for implementing load-balancing mechanisms and call throttling to effectively manage and regulate the utilization of these services.

Data foundations

Data plays a vital role in the field of AI and machine learning, with data scientists tasked with building ML models devoting roughly 80 per cent of their time to handling the data used for training and testing. This responsibility encompasses a range of tasks, including selecting the appropriate dataset, cleansing the data, selecting relevant features, mitigating data biases, enhancing data quality, labelling data and, when necessary, creating synthetic data.

Over the course of several decades, data management has undergone a transformative journey, progressing from transactional databases to data warehouses, big data repositories, data lakes, data fabrics and now data meshes. The underlying objective of these advancements has consistently revolved around aggregating enterprise data, enabling diverse data consumers to interact with it according to their specific needs.

Facilitating the task of data science significantly is the provision of easy access to a centralized repository of data, accompanied by robust tools for data manipulation and transformation, commonly referred to as data pre-processing.

It's crucial to acknowledge that the landscape of data strategy and foundational infrastructure is in a constant state of flux, evolving as part of ongoing initiatives aimed at enhancing data management, streamlining infrastructure, migrating to cloud environments and harnessing the latest architectural designs and technologies.

Going back to the 1990s and early 2000s, the advent of big data technologies revolutionized the consolidation of data from multiple sources, enabling more computationally intensive analytics and reporting. The domain of data management and infrastructure has continued to evolve at an accelerated pace, with a significant boost from the introduction of cloud computing in 2006 through AWS, particularly with its Elastic Compute EC2 service. Subsequently, we have witnessed a continued progression in data infrastructures, marked by milestones such as the emergence of data lakes in 2011 and the more recent development of the data mesh concept in 2019.

Four: Data science frameworks

The term data science relates to the functions of designing, prototyping, building, testing, deploying and monitoring machine learning models. While the term was first coined back in 1974, it only became widely used after a publication in 2001.[1]

It is now used to refer to the practice, the process, the people and the teams that specifically work on machine learning and artificial intelligence technologies.

Most organizations will set up a dedicated data science team(s) to support the required analytics, insights and predictive capabilities required from the rest of the IT department/business functional areas.

Data science teams can often be in direct conflict with the rest of the IT teams/division, due to a widely different approach, the need for rapid experimentation, and unexpected results and timelines to develop reliable and robust predictive models.

It requires the CTO/IT director and the rest of the senior management team to understand the different processes, the dependence of data and data quality, and the potential for unpredictable results or levels of accuracy that may be unacceptable.

A strong collaboration between the head of data science and the IT director/CTO is required to smooth the path to production for any data science team and the models they produce, especially for the first few implementations.

While historically the process of data science has lacked appropriate tools to support a professional approach, much has changed in recent years, with more formal structures, frameworks, processes and tools available to allow a scaled capability for any data science team.

Below we detail the core aspects that can support a data science team to work in a formal and mature setting that will align well with the rest of the IT department.

The practice of data science will leverage a top-level framework that sets out the different aspects, processes and considerations needed. Some frameworks will focus mostly on the technical aspects of data science. However, we prefer to use a more holistic framework, as shown in Figure 9.2, which factors in several different areas and considerations as shown by the four individual views of the framework given in Figure 9.3. These are the main areas that any data science team should consider as it works towards building robust and responsible models and a mature and capable data science practice.

FIGURE 9.2   The data science framework

BUSINESS VALUE & AI STRATEGY ALIGNMENT		
DATA SCIENCE WORKFLOW PROCESS	OP MODEL & ORG STRUCTURE	AUDIT & ETHICS
TECHNICAL FRAMEWORK & TOOLS		
PEOPLE – SKILLS CAPABILITY AND CULTURE		
GOVERNANCE – DATA & ALGORITHMS		
DATA FOUNDATIONS		
INFRASTRUCTURE / CLOUD PLATFORM		

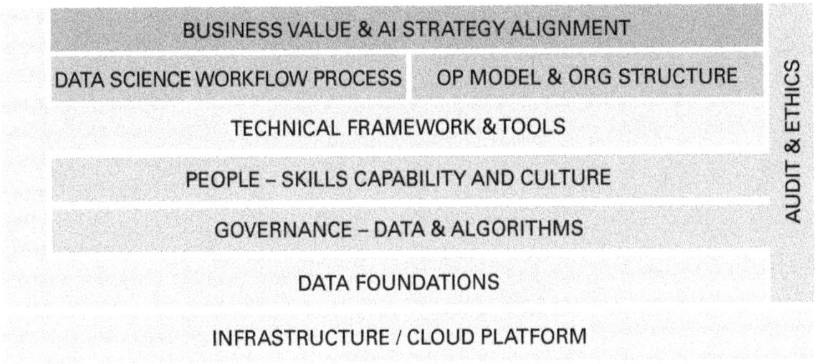

Data science workflow and process

A typical workflow or pipeline for developing ML models is shown in Figure 9.4 and starts from the design through to deployment, monitoring and retraining. This is an iterative process on both the development and production sides, requiring a series of checkpoints and a tollgate before moving to the next step in the workflow but also requiring the need to revise and improve (via the feedback loops) to achieve the best possible performance.

The checkpoints and tollgate are an opportunity to review the process and ensure the development is aligned with the core AI principles and following appropriate guidelines on AI ethics.

Most companies, consultancies and AI vendors will have a very similar approach to the data science framework and process; there may be differences in implementation and the tools they use, but fundamentally the approach will be the same.

Five: Skills and talent

One of the most significant hurdles in the process of AI adoption revolves around the acquisition of the requisite skills and

FIGURE 9.3 Data science framework: four focus areas

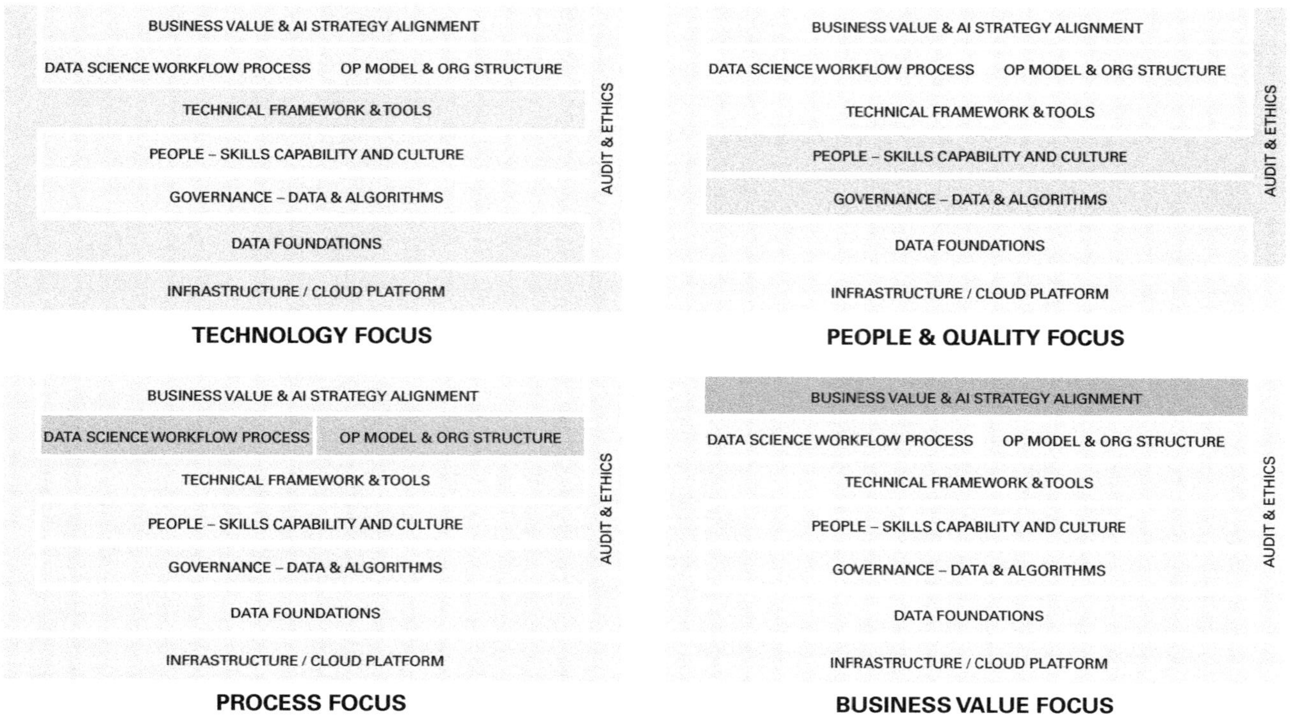

TECHNOLOGY FOCUS

- BUSINESS VALUE & AI STRATEGY ALIGNMENT
- OP MODEL & ORG STRUCTURE
- DATA SCIENCE WORKFLOW PROCESS
- TECHNICAL FRAMEWORK & TOOLS
- PEOPLE – SKILLS CAPABILITY AND CULTURE
- GOVERNANCE – DATA & ALGORITHMS
- DATA FOUNDATIONS
- INFRASTRUCTURE / CLOUD PLATFORM
- AUDIT & ETHICS

PROCESS FOCUS

- BUSINESS VALUE & AI STRATEGY ALIGNMENT
- OP MODEL & ORG STRUCTURE
- DATA SCIENCE WORKFLOW PROCESS
- TECHNICAL FRAMEWORK & TOOLS
- PEOPLE – SKILLS CAPABILITY AND CULTURE
- GOVERNANCE – DATA & ALGORITHMS
- DATA FOUNDATIONS
- INFRASTRUCTURE / CLOUD PLATFORM
- AUDIT & ETHICS

PEOPLE & QUALITY FOCUS

- BUSINESS VALUE & AI STRATEGY ALIGNMENT
- OP MODEL & ORG STRUCTURE
- DATA SCIENCE WORKFLOW PROCESS
- TECHNICAL FRAMEWORK & TOOLS
- PEOPLE – SKILLS CAPABILITY AND CULTURE
- GOVERNANCE – DATA & ALGORITHMS
- DATA FOUNDATIONS
- INFRASTRUCTURE / CLOUD PLATFORM
- AUDIT & ETHICS

BUSINESS VALUE FOCUS

- BUSINESS VALUE & AI STRATEGY ALIGNMENT
- OP MODEL & ORG STRUCTURE
- DATA SCIENCE WORKFLOW PROCESS
- TECHNICAL FRAMEWORK & TOOLS
- PEOPLE – SKILLS CAPABILITY AND CULTURE
- GOVERNANCE – DATA & ALGORITHMS
- DATA FOUNDATIONS
- INFRASTRUCTURE / CLOUD PLATFORM
- AUDIT & ETHICS

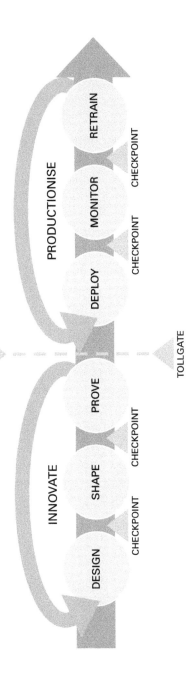

FIGURE 9.4   Data science pipeline/workflow

expertise, particularly those individuals who possess both a deep understanding of the subject matter and experience in AI. Although enlisting external teams with a background in AI can expedite progress, many organizations seek to explore strategies for cultivating internal capabilities that will serve them over the long term. This transition is typically a gradual, well-planned process that entails shifting responsibilities from external teams to in-house resources over time.

The development of skills and talent in this context aligns with the broader stages of AI adoption. During the initial phases, such as innovation and early development and scaling, external assistance and guidance are often invaluable, if not essential, for achieving successful outcomes. As the organization accumulates more knowledge and experience, the transition towards internal resource ownership becomes a natural progression.

Hidden talent

Often in an organization of a certain size, you will be able to find people with educational or practical knowledge and experience of machine learning that could be utilized as you progress with your AI adoption. The first stage is to identify these people by setting up a community of practice (CoP) for AI. You will also surface people who are particularly interested in the field of AI and machine learning and looking to reskill into a data science role. Identifying these resources and aligning them with early AI innovation projects will help to build your long-term capabilities in this area.

Training and education

A crucial aspect of supporting staff in adapting to any new technology is the provision of comprehensive staff education and training. This extends not only to the onboarding process for new staff members but also to the ongoing awareness-building efforts for the existing workforce as the integration of AI within the organization continues to grow.

AI AWARENESS TRAINING FOR EMPLOYEES
All employees involved in AI-related activities are likely to be required to undergo AI awareness training as part of their onboarding process. The training programme will cover an introduction to AI and cover the fundamental principles of AI, including ethics, fairness, transparency, bias mitigation and data privacy. Employees will also be required to participate in periodic refresher courses to stay updated on the evolving fields of AI, responsible usage, standards and organizational policies.

CONTINUOUS LEARNING AND PROFESSIONAL DEVELOPMENT
Most companies will offer access to training as part of their continuous learning and professional development programmes. These will allow you to extend your knowledge and skills in both technical areas and the soft skills needed to work in the field of AI.

TRAINING RESOURCES
Abundant resources are available for AI and ML training, with a significant amount of them being freely accessible. The major cloud platforms offer a wide range of training materials and educational resources. These resources empower anyone to deepen their understanding of the ML products and services available and gain insights into the practical ways to use them.

Community activities

In the early days, weeks and months of AI adoption, setting up communities to support the initial activities will be vitally important to coordinate efforts, help share the experiences, celebrate the initial achievements and build internal knowledge on the topic.

I recommend designating a few individuals within the organization as 'AI champions'. These individuals will be responsible for promoting AI best practice, including ethics awareness, answering questions and serving as a resource for adoption guidance within their respective teams.

AI champions will collaborate with the AI governance committee and the AI ethics officer to provide input on AI adoption considerations and contribute to the development of AI best practices.

They will also get involved in the CoP to help disseminate information and showcase quick wins and processes with the wider organization.

Many organizations will look to set up a CoP or working group. This is often a great way to share initial work and proofs of concept, and discuss tools and solutions. CoPs can be used to showcase work done in different parts of the organization, help troubleshoot issues, determine standards and allow people across the organization to share information and approaches to help accelerate adoption.

Many folks will join this CoP to learn and improve understanding, allowing the whole organization to feel part of the AI adoption journey.

It could be that you already have a suitable forum to use and simply need to expand the scope of topics included to cover your AI and ML adoption journey. However, for such an important and complex subject, having something dedicated shows the organization how seriously you are taking this matter.

Six: Culture of innovation

Fostering an innovative culture within an organization stands as a critical pillar for the sustained success of any innovation programme, and this responsibility falls squarely on the shoulders of the leadership team.

In contrast to other forms of technology development, the realm of data science and machine learning doesn't follow a linear path; it demands a significant degree of experimentation and trial and error. This unpredictability can be viewed as frustrating, complicating project management and planning. These frustrations often surface, whether employing Agile or Waterfall project management methodologies, and can potentially lead to challenging conflicts between the head or lead data scientist, technology director and project or programme managers.

To nurture an innovative culture, it's imperative to eliminate the fear of failure during the early stages of AI adoption. This is precisely why we advocate for taking a portfolio approach to AI innovation.

Furthermore, when an organization undertakes digital transformation, it reaps additional benefits beyond the successful development and deployment of early high-priority use-cases. These advantages encompass the tacit experience and knowledge acquired by the team and the confidence to implement other AI use-cases.

Equally important is involving the entire organization in the innovation and adoption journey. Some areas may need to wait patiently until the priority use-cases are delivered before they can also benefit from enhanced productivity and functional improvements. However, there might be quick wins that allow other parts of the company to experience the culture of innovation and its progress.

The introduction of AI primarily aims at enhancing productivity, enabling growth and expanding capabilities rather than solely focusing on cost-cutting and reductions. This positive messaging and its reinforcement play a pivotal role in strengthening the culture of innovation and fostering acceptance of the technology at hand.

Moreover, innovation extends beyond technology; it encompasses people and processes. AI serves as a transformative tool, automating mundane tasks and affording individuals more time to engage in higher-value and more gratifying work.

Seven: Organizational structure and governance

The selection of the right organization structure for data science team(s) will depend on the size of the organization, how it currently operates with its technology department and the maturity of its AI adoption.

While this serves as a blueprint for how to organize your AI/ML team(s) over time, there will be other factors that influence the specific setup and preference within your company. We will provide details of each option of structure, with the benefits and challenges of each, so it will help the senior management team decide the best structure at the current time.

Depending on the size of company and how the current functions of IT are organized, the structure and operations may remain at the first stage; however, for others the model may change and introduce the Centre of Excellence (CoE) model, shown as stages two to four of Figure 9.5.

Structural options

As a summary, Figure 9.5 gives the five main approaches. For each we will explore the reasons for using that structure and how it will likely evolve into the next, starting at the left with the central approach and transitioning over time through different versions of the CoE model.

AI adoption maturity

Based on AI adoption maturity, I have divided the structural options into two phases. The first is focused on the early stages of AI adoption, with major emphasis on innovation, proof of value, proof of concept or minimum viable product

FIGURE 9.5   Operating model structures ordered by adoption maturity

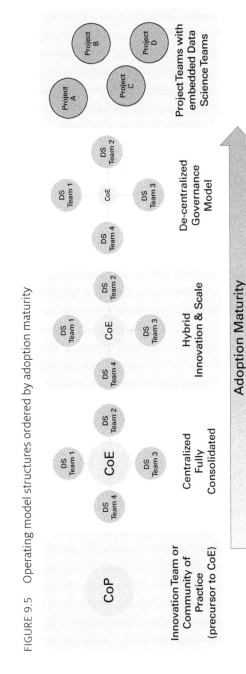

development. The second phase moves from initial innovation to a more structured approach to apply AI in specific areas and functions, which aligns with the build and scale stage of the AI adoption journey.

Often the first phase of AI adoption comes from individuals exploring its use in a particular area or use-case; these small pockets of AI innovation can be unplanned and disorganized from a firm-wide perspective.

The key here is to nurture the organizational desire to innovate with AI technologies and support the innovation culture. This is a great time to set up a CoP or working group to help surface all the activity and showcase these initial innovation successes.

The key for the organization is to understand what is being done and to maximize the learning and knowledge gained.

There are several ways to set up a data science team or teams within your organization. Large organizations are likely to need multiple teams spread across the different departments. The way a company organizes its data science teams will also change as its experience and maturity evolves.

The four standard models of organizational structures are:

Centralized: In this approach, data science teams are centralized within the organization and provide support and expertise to all departments. This can help to ensure consistency in data science practices and methodologies across the organization.

Decentralized: In this approach, each department has its own data science team, allowing them to focus on department-specific data science initiatives and projects. This can be particularly useful for departments with unique data science needs and goals.

Hybrid: In this approach, there is a mix of centralized and decentralized data science teams, with a central team providing overall guidance and support and department-specific teams focusing on department-specific initiatives. This can be a useful compromise between the centralized and decentralized approaches, allowing for both consistency and flexibility. Often referred to as the hub-and-spoke model.

Project-based: In this approach, data science teams are organized around specific projects, with team members coming from different departments as needed. This can be useful for cross-functional projects that require expertise from multiple departments.

It is common that when a company starts exploring the use of AI, it will have a very fragmented and decentralized setup, often happening organically and aligning to the current structure of the organization. Over time this may change to one or more of the structures specified above. Each structure has well-defined benefits and drawbacks that need to be understood; the transition between structural models can also provide a mix of opportunities and challenges.

While the natural focus is on data science teams, it is possible to have other tribes, covering different types of data analytics and insights. For example, in some industries, the business users, as well as the technology department, might have expertise with different aspects of analytics and predictive algorithms. Different tribes will have distinctive preferences for tools and frameworks and might work in very different delivery modes. These cultural variations may be incompatible to combine without some understanding and considerations.

Governance

The field of AI ethics and governance is both expansive and complex, and given the limited concrete guidance from regulators, each company is tasked with establishing its own best practices. While various government bodies and institutions have published guidelines and frameworks that serve as valuable references (some of which we will mention later), it ultimately falls on each company to define how they will govern the use of

AI and shape their ethical stance regarding different facets of AI adoption.

The initial step in this journey involves establishing a set of core AI principles that the company will adhere to. These principles serve as the foundation upon which all AI-related activities and developments are built. They provide a clear framework for aligning AI initiatives with ethical considerations and mitigating regulatory, legal and other potential business risks.

The management of AI governance plays a pivotal role in ensuring that all AI use-cases and developments remain in sync with the core AI principles and related policies. It encompasses a systematic approach to guaranteeing that AI implementations do not introduce regulatory, legal or operational risks. It's worth noting that AI governance need not be a standalone entity but can seamlessly integrate into the broader context of IT governance.

Rather than creating separate forums, committees or review panels exclusively for AI projects or applications, it is recommended to incorporate AI governance into the existing IT governance structure. By doing so, companies can streamline the process, reduce redundancy and ensure that AI governance aligns with the overall organizational governance framework. This integrated approach facilitates a more cohesive and efficient management of AI ethics and governance across the organization.

Eight: Planning, vendors and partners

Planning

Large-scale implementations and technical change require detailed planning and coordination across the organization, as often many separate projects are running in parallel that can potentially overlap and impact one another. None of this is new for IT departments and any AI project or deployment should be simply seen as just another IT project, with all the same checks, reviews, synchronization and detailed implementation planning as any other.

What can be slightly different from other IT projects is the need for more ongoing monitoring and retraining of any deployed ML models to ensure the correct level of performance and accuracy over time.

Partnering for success

One method of reducing the challenges of AI adoption is to work with a partner organization that has extensive experience in implementing AI. For large-scale implementations it might require the combination of an AI consultancy together with one or more vendor firms that have specialist platforms or applications that are needed.

AI CONSULTANCIES

There are many different technology consultancies that can help with AI implementations. They will range in size, industries covered and specific AI capability experience, so selection is important to ensure the right fit with what you are looking to achieve.

AI VENDORS – PLATFORMS AND APPLICATIONS

Selection of vendors who either provide some of the core infrastructure and platforms or deliver more functional applications can be very challenging, simply because there is a significant choice. There are thousands of vendors providing various AI capabilities, each with specific functionality, alignment to underlying technology footprints and expertise in different areas of AI.

Often companies will use an AI consultancy to help determine the correct AI architecture and vendor selection to match the company needs with the capabilities of the platform, applications, frameworks and tools.

ACADEMIC COLLABORATION

For early-stage innovation work, collaborating with an academic institution could be a method for organizations to get started on their AI adoption roadmap.

TECHNOLOGY SELECTION (FRAMEWORKS AND TOOLS)

As most firms will already have a technology footprint in place, some of the decisions will most likely align with the current infrastructure. For example, if a firm is already using one of the cloud providers, it is unlikely to want to use a different one for its AI/ML use-cases. However, while some of the major decisions might be relatively easy, there is still a vast array of data science frameworks and tools to select from. This might start very organically, with different data science teams trying different ones and seeing which works best for them. This may be a good way to start, but it will potentially cause problems later, especially if you have multiple data science teams working in different parts of the organization – this is when standardization becomes more important.

Nine: Managing an AI-powered workforce

As an increasing number of businesses embrace artificial intelligence and other emerging technologies, the role of the modern business leader is undergoing a transformation. A significant challenge faced by these leaders is the management of a workforce comprising both human employees and intelligent AI-powered technologies.

Leading a workforce driven by AI can be both demanding and rewarding. By skilfully managing the transition to an AI-powered workplace, focusing on upskilling and reskilling their team, and embracing a leadership style marked by transparency and collaboration, leaders can cultivate a team that excels in productivity and engagement. By harnessing the advantages of AI while preserving a robust human presence, they can steer your organization towards success and maintain a competitive edge in the swiftly evolving business landscape.

The benefits of an AI-powered workforce

A workforce augmented with AI tools and applications can become superhuman. Organizations that encourage and enable the workforce to gain such advantage will benefit in many different ways:

1 **Automation and productivity gains:** For one, it can help to automate repetitive tasks, freeing up your employees to focus on more value-added work. Automating the mundane helps free up time for more productive tasks. We have also seen how generative AI provides major productivity improvements across many business functions.

2 **Decision making:** AI can also assist with data analysis and decision making, helping your team to make more informed and efficient decisions. It also typically leads to more real-time-based decisions, also enabling decisions to be made by those closer to the problem.

3 **Customer service:** Additionally, AI can help to improve customer service and satisfaction, as well as increase productivity and efficiency. It can also provide a more personalized and individual service and enable improved cross-sell and up-sell opportunities.

4 **More challenging problems:** AI can free up time for employees to spend more time solving the more difficult and challenging problems.

Managing the transition to an AI-powered workplace

However, transitioning to an AI-powered workplace can also be challenging. Some employees may be hesitant to adopt new technologies or may be concerned about the potential impact on their job security. It's important that leaders manage these concerns and ensure that their teams feel supported during the transition. Here are a few strategies:

1 **Communicate clearly:** Teams need to understand the reasons behind the adoption of AI and how it will benefit the organization as a whole.
2 **Provide training:** Training and support to help teams learn how to use the new technologies effectively.
3 **Address concerns about job security:** Retraining or other support to help employees adapt to the new environment.
4 **Emphasize the value of human skills:** While AI can automate certain tasks, there are many tasks that require human judgment and creativity. Teams should be reassured of the importance of these skills and should continue developing them.

Upskilling and reskilling teams

As AI and other emerging technologies continue to advance, it's important for business leaders to ensure that their teams have the skills and knowledge to thrive in this new environment. This may involve upskilling current employees as well as bringing in new talent with the necessary skills.

With the growing prevalence of generative AI tools, the skill of prompt engineering, to maximize the performance of these technologies and get the best possible results, is becoming a key non-technical skill that some resources within the firm may need training and educational support in.

Here are a few strategies you can use to improve the skills of your team:

Offer training and development opportunities: Provide your team with the resources and support they need to learn new skills and stay up to date with the latest technologies.

Encourage continuous learning: Encourage your team to take an active role in their own learning and create a culture that values ongoing development.

Hire for potential: When recruiting new talent, focus on individuals who have the potential to learn and adapt quickly, rather than just those who have specific skills or experience

Leading an AI-powered team

Leaders need to find the right balance between leveraging the benefits of AI and maintaining a strong human element. Here are a few tips for effectively leading an AI-powered team:

Foster collaboration: Encourage collaboration between human and AI team members and create an environment where they can work together effectively.

Emphasize transparency: Make sure the team understands how AI is being used, and the limitations and capabilities of the technology. This can help to build trust and prevent misunderstandings.

Encourage creativity: While AI can automate certain tasks, it's important to encourage creativity and human input in decision making and problem solving.

Encourage your team to come up with new ideas and approaches and create a culture that values innovation:

Manage expectations: Make sure your team has clear goals and expectations and provide regular feedback and support to help them stay on track.

Lead by example: As a leader, it's important to model the behaviour you want to see in your team. This includes being open to new technologies and approaches and showing a willingness to learn and adapt.

Benefits of an AI-powered business

Moving your business to be an AI-first company requires significant cultural changes, as many of the processes and procedures will need to be modified to properly benefit from the full advantages of utilizing AI across the organization.

Core to this cultural change is the move towards real-time analysis and decision making. Not only does this put pressure on the organization to react quickly to the latest information, it also potentially allows more people in the company to have access to such knowledge and therefore make changes to plans and activities much more quickly than before.

REAL-TIME ANALYSIS AND DECISION MAKING

Real-time analysis and decision making can offer many benefits to businesses, but it also poses a number of challenges. Some of the key opportunities and challenges include the following.

Opportunities:

1 **Improved efficiency:** Real-time analysis allows businesses to make decisions quickly, which can lead to more efficient operations and faster reaction times to market changes or other events.

2 **Better customer service:** Real-time analysis can help businesses to better understand and respond to customer needs, leading to improved customer satisfaction and retention.

3 **Increased competitiveness:** Real-time decision making can give businesses a competitive edge, allowing them to respond more quickly and effectively to changing market conditions.

4 **Automation of processes:** Using real-time capabilities allows for automation of processes, reducing human errors and allowing decision to be made faster.

Challenges:

1 **Complexity:** Real-time analysis often involves processing large amounts of data in complex ways, which can be technically challenging.

2 **Data quality:** Analytics relies on high-quality data and accurate data collection, which can be difficult to ensure, especially for real-time applications.

3 **Technical infrastructure:** Real-time analysis requires sophisticated technical infrastructure, including robust data storage and processing capabilities.

4 **Latency:** The delay in data processing can affect the real-time decision-making process.

5 **Transparency:** Explainable AI becomes increasingly important for real-time decision making as the complexity of the process increases and the transparency of the decision-making process is crucial.

6 **Cybersecurity:** Ensuring the security of real-time data is crucial as it can be targeted by hackers

7 **Privacy:** Ensuring the privacy of data is becoming increasingly important for real-time decision making

Overall, real-time analysis and decision making can be challenging, but it also offers many benefits. Businesses that are able to successfully implement these technologies will be well positioned to take advantage of the opportunities they offer.

Final thoughts

The importance now of AI for businesses cannot be overstated; it is becoming an increasingly critical part of the technology landscape and has the ability to totally transform business strategy, opportunity, risks and models. Such a significant capability, which can have a major impact on the success or failure of a business, deserves the investment of time and resource to define the strategic approach to its implementation and use.

Understanding the AI strategy of a company, and its relative stage of adoption, will be very insightful for everyone working to help make the vision a reality. As the adoption and maturity advances, new career opportunities will materialize and allow you to advance your role and responsibilities as the company scales its use of AI across the organization.

While having a well-defined approach to the adoption of AI is a worthwhile investment in the business plan and strategy of any company, it is very possible that at the early stages of AI innovation and discovery, firms just want to try and see, learn by doing and experiment with the technology to see what is possible and how it might benefit them in practical terms.

Within any industry there will be leaders and followers – those who wish to invest in innovation and seize any opportunity to gain competitive advantage, and those who prefer to see how the sector will mature before committing too much too soon. Regardless of the speed, the tide is turning and the majority of companies will need to benefit from the application of AI.

Note

1   Cleveland, W S (2001) Data Science: An action plan for expanding the technical areas of the field of statistics, www.researchgate.net/publication/2367122_Data_Science_An_Action_Plan_for_Expanding_the_Technical_Areas_of_the_Field_of_Statistics (archived at https://perma.cc/5LMN-ZECS)

CHAPTER TEN

Implementing AI

Despite the rapid rise and mass market appeal of AI over the last few months with generative AI, implementing AI at scale within an organization is not as simple as it might seem at first glance. There are many challenges and obstacles to overcome as AI adoption moves from the early stages of innovation, running proof-of-value or proof-of-concept, to transitioning through the various phases of the software development lifecycle (SDLC) into a production environment.

Deploying into a live environment for AI and ML applications isn't the end of the story; ongoing monitoring and potentially retraining are required to keep the performance at an acceptable level, as data drift can make these models perform poorly over time.

A lack of focus on these issues can be disastrous to the reputation of AI within an organization if they are not properly managed and controlled. We know that IT projects can be problematic for various reasons, and ML deployments are just as complex if not more, especially on the first production deployment.

This chapter provides details of the various options available for implementing AI solutions, as well as the considerations and best practices associated with each approach. This will also showcase other possible career options across the entire ecosystem.

12 challenges of AI adoption

Before we look at implementation approaches, it might be useful to better understand some of the challenges that scaled implementations face throughout the process of developing and deploying.

Organizations big and small are starting the process of exploration of artificial intelligence. Some of these companies are well advanced in their adoption of intelligent technologies, but many are just at the beginning of this challenging adoption journey.

I have identified 12 top challenges for the adoption of AI at scale that we see many firms experiencing at some point in the early years of AI adoption. Many occur when the organization moves from the innovation lab to production-ready live applications:

1 Conflicts between IT departments and data science teams (sometimes the data science work is done initially within the business lines/business users).
2 Scaling AI challenges with multiple data science teams.
3 Middle management fighting over ownership of data science.
4 Business users not trusting the technology (taking six months to approve).
5 Identifying the business use-cases for AI and ML technologies.
6 Understanding the ROI for investing in ML and automation capabilities.

7 Confusion with the number of vendors/products/tools and platforms.

8 Data bias and ethical issues slowing acceptance and adoption.

9 Correctly defining the governance model for monitoring and control.

10 Changes in culture and organizational structure needed across the organization with the democratization of data (information and knowledge).

11 Need to skill existing teams to better understand how AI/ML works.

12 Need for a top-level vision and strategy for how the business will become AI-first

While I have identified 12 of the top (most common) challenges for AI adoption, there are many more potential challenges that can derail your own AI implementation plans. Part of defining an AI strategy will be to identify the areas that need focus and support to ensure smooth implementation paths.

Overcoming implementation challenges

As highlighted in the previous section, there are a wide range of challenges to AI implementation; these vary in area and will have very different methods to overcome them.

Some of these challenges relate to having defined and actioned an AI strategy. Some will relate to the way you set up teams within the organization to work on AI/ML. Other challenges relate to how AI adoption is managed and communicated within the firm. Additional challenges can be addressed with a training and educational plan.

More challenges come from a lack of IT governance and control for data science work or a limited appreciation of the ethical and data bias considerations. The monitoring and ongoing performance review of deployed ML models is also an important area that is somewhat different from more standard IT applications.

Ultimately, there are many areas that need proper consideration to ensure the smooth implementation of AI applications and systems. Without the proper frameworks and tools to support AI implementations there are many potential risks and pitfalls that need to be navigated.

Implementation approaches

There are so many different potential options here, which I will expand on in the following sections, but let us just reflect on the top-level considerations first to frame it better and help us understand why it's such a complex decision.

The first aspect to consider is the huge amount of choice available. There are literally thousands of AI vendors and start-up companies all producing AI applications that can solve many of the problems most businesses will want to solve with AI. The vendors of existing products are also racing to add AI capabilities into their own product functionality, but often this is not as transparent as one would like. You also have most of the technology and some of the business consultancies offering capabilities to build AI platforms and applications.

You also have all the cloud platform providers having a range of building blocks for AI and ML build, including many pre-trained models that can be leveraged as a starting point for many of the problems you might be wanting to solve.

Understanding what is available and the detailed functionality is a complex vendor selection and due diligence process at best.

This is then made even more complex because this is not a static situation. New models are being released on a weekly basis, with new functionality and capabilities, so much so that this is a moving target that is as fast as it's ever been.

While selecting a vendor solution might be the answer (or maybe part of the answer), there are other options available. If you have a strong IT department already, there may be options to build out a small data science team to work on the early use-cases selected.

Internal AI development

The most desirable long-term situation will be to have your own data science team building and supporting any and all ML models used within your organization. It may be possible to create this team from existing resources, a combination of hidden talent who already have experience and interest in AI work and those who are keen to retrain and reskill as data scientists. Otherwise, you can look to hire in a few experienced people to seed the team and then gradually grow from there.

Building an internal AI team(s)

Having an internal AI team will give you the highest degree of control and flexibility in what is built and how it operates, easier to align with your existing data management and technology footprint. This also enables much closer collaboration with the business users and the wider IT team to ensure functional and non-functional requirement alignment.

However, there are challenges with this approach. Talent acquisition can be problematic due to the high demand and sparse supply of skilled data scientists. Also, if your team is small, retention may also be difficult in the medium to long term. You may also need a more senior data scientist or factional CAIO to help set up and guide the overall practice during the early stages.

Many companies have gone down this road, setting up initial teams from the very start, and have seen much success.

Custom AI development

One of the main advantages of having an internal team is to maximize the ability to create bespoke or customized models based on internal data that you may not want to expose externally. The tech firms who are building the foundational LLM (large language model) have now started to provide the tools and capabilities to create customized models while respecting data privacy. But this still needs expertise, and an initial team who are closest to understanding the data you wish to use to create a bespoke model is the most sensible approach.

For LLMs, we have seen a number of approaches emerge for tailoring models, from a technique called grounding, which leverages a co-pilot orchestration/coordination program together with access to an internal knowledge graph or database, to fine-tuning or refinement learning that uses additional training data to create a customized model.

Bespoke builds are often needed for complex tasks that are very industry/company specific, requiring the use of internal commercially sensitive data to train a custom model.

AI consultancies

While the largest of companies will have the money and people to set up their own data science team, they may still find it useful to leverage the help and support of a consultancy firm that has deep experience with delivering AI at scale (and many large corporations do use consultancies to support their adoption of AI). Many SME companies have the problems and desire to use AI, but might be lacking in their internal capacity to do so. Using a consultancy to augment the team to get started is often the best way to accelerate the initial deployments, to secure early wins that will help communicate to the entire company the level of investment and desire to adopt AI technologies to secure the future of the firm.

Working with AI consultancies

Collaborating with an external AI consultancy firm can work in different ways. It might be to help determine the best AI strategy for your company, or you just want to get straight into the delivery of your first few AI use-cases. Both strategic and delivery advisory work can be in scope for some AI consultancies, while others will focus on one or the other. Data science as a service is a common option, providing a data science team to build initial analytics and predictive models as prioritized.

Engagement with consultancies will often need members of the internal team to act as liaisons, supporting and managing the work required from them.

Because consultancies typically work with many companies, across many different industries, they can bring best-practice standards, new ideas and solutions that you may not have previously thought about. This richness of experience and knowledge coming from consultancies can be a real boost to the way you view the benefits of AI adoption.

Vendor products and services

The AI vendor landscape is enormous, with thousands of products and solutions available across all parts of the business value chain. The choice is often unmanageable, with any one company unlikely to be able to assess all possible options available.

Here too is where an AI consultancy might be able to support, having a wider knowledge of more vendor tools than an individual firm might experience.

Any vendor due diligence needs to start by properly understanding the requirements (both functional and non-functional) in the short term and longer term too. This can then be used as a method of evaluation with a few potential candidate solutions taken from a larger set of potentials that have been filtered by a paper-based comparison of known features and functions.

Leveraging vendor AI solutions

There is an increasing number of AI vendors, providing a wide range of software products and capabilities that can be used to solve specific problems across the business value chain using AI and machine learning. This means you won't necessarily need to build a solution from scratch, rather simply integrate one of these vendor applications into your overall technology footprint, connecting it to your data and fitting it into existing processes.

Also, many of the current software products being used by companies will be updated (if they haven't already) to include some form of AI/ML capabilities and functionality that users can benefit from. Potential issues include that the specific functions don't align with your own requirements, you need to wait until the functions you need are developed and deployed, you need to upgrade to a different subscription level to access the AI functionality, or the functionality you need isn't going to be built and integrated into the product.

The hybrid approach

The most likely and most beneficial methodology will be to implement a hybrid team leveraging the best of each of the previously detailed approaches. Here you can seed your internal team with external expertise from an AI consultancy and accelerate adoption with use of some vendor products and tools.

I have seen this work well, using a consultancy to set up a data science team and then gradually phasing in internal resources and training them up, with the aim to eventually build a fully operational internal data science team that can continue the work started by the consultancy.

Hybrid AI implementation strategies

There are many factors to consider, including the size of the team needed, the amount of work anticipated and the degree of complexity with the models required. These factors then help determine the correct shape of the hybrid team, both at the beginning and when the team reaches maturity. Once this picture is formed, a plan can be devised to facilitate the recruitment and ramp-up of resources to align with the target.

As part of the hybrid team and the implementation plan, appropriate time and resources should be reserved for training up of any company resources that are looking to reskill as data scientists.

If the hybrid team plan is well devised and implemented, the team will evolve into an internal AI team, allowing the consultancy firm that seeded the team to exit.

Final thoughts

Building and using simple forms of AI can be deceptively easy. The big tech firms have invested heavily in tools to make the process as easy as possible, allowing not just IT professionals to build them, but putting the ability in the hands of business users too.

This might create a false sense of security, with management in particular assuming that all forms of AI are going to be this easy and inexpensive.

The better you need the AI to perform, and the more challenging the problem, the more complex the solution needs to be. And with complexity comes increased cost and time, and the need for more specific data to train bespoke models.

CHAPTER ELEVEN

Governance, ethics and safety

It is only in recent years, with the real-world applications of AI becoming more widespread and the potential for misaligned decisions from biased models seemingly more significant, that the topics of governance, ethics and safety have become elevated into the most senior discussions and considerations for the implementation and control of AI applications and systems.

The terminology has evolved over the last few years; initially it was responsible AI, then ethical AI, now the focus is on safe and trustworthy AI. They all mean pretty much the same thing, as the topic tends to cover the full range of concerns.

Parts of the industry, together with various institutions and governments, are calling out, and in some cases defining, the legal framework to regulate the AI industry to ensure all of these concerns are managed and controlled in appropriate ways based on the level of risk from different applications and models.

Many of the larger companies, too, have defined their own governance and usage policies, implementing workflows to ensure proper review and approval of AI-based applications.

This is a new area for AI, part of its own journey of maturity to provide a level of security, trust and confidence that the AI applications we use have been built with the right checks and balances to ensure fair and transparent decision making.

In this chapter we will look at each part of this area in more detail and highlight the potential roles and career paths that are emerging.

Governance

AI governance and regulation encompasses the establishment of policies, procedures and frameworks to oversee and control the development, deployment and utilization of artificial intelligence. The primary objective of AI governance and regulation is to ensure that AI is created and employed in a manner that upholds ethical standards, responsibility and alignment with societal values.

AI governance presents a multitude of challenges and considerations, including:

1 **Ethical AI development and usage:** This entails ensuring that AI systems are designed and used in a manner that respects human rights, privacy and dignity, while also preventing the perpetuation or amplification of biases or discrimination.

2 **Transparency and accountability of AI:** This necessitates the implementation of transparency measures in AI systems' decision-making processes, along with mechanisms for holding these systems accountable for their actions.

3 **Safety and reliability of AI:** The focus is on ensuring that AI systems operate safely and reliably, with measures in place to mitigate associated risks.

4 **Fair and responsible AI deployment:** This involves guaranteeing the equitable distribution of AI benefits and minimizing negative impacts on areas such as employment, education, finance and society.

Various approaches and initiatives have been proposed or put into practice to address these challenges. These include codes of ethics, regulatory frameworks and industry self-regulation. Effective AI governance and regulation requires collaboration among stakeholders in the AI ecosystem, including governments, industry players, academia and civil society. However, a significant challenge lies in the fact that while many governments have issued papers and guidelines in this domain, they tend to be high-level, leaving companies to decipher how to achieve compliance. As a result, different organizations, even within the same industry, may adopt slightly distinct approaches.

Ethics

Ethics and data bias are important considerations in data science, as the data and models that we create and use can have significant impacts on society and individuals. It is important for data scientists to be aware of the ethical considerations and challenges that may arise in their work, and to take steps to address them.

Some common issues that data scientists may encounter include bias in data collection and analysis, privacy and security concerns, and the responsible use of AI. Techniques for addressing bias in data and models include data cleaning and normalization, fair representation learning and the use of unbiased evaluation metrics.

Many large firms will already have in place a responsible AI framework that helps to guide the teams of data scientists around the many challenges and potential pitfalls of ethical AI.

This is a large and complex area of AI, which could easily be the topic of a whole book, but some of the main areas to be considered include:

1 **Bias and fairness:** One of the key concerns in AI ethics is the issue of bias and fairness. AI systems can exhibit bias if the

data they are trained on is biased or if the algorithms used to develop them are biased. This can lead to unfair or discriminatory outcomes for certain groups of people.

2 **Transparency and explainability:** Another important topic in AI ethics is the issue of transparency and explainability. Many AI systems are complex and difficult to understand, making it hard for users and regulators to understand how they work and what factors influence their decisions. This can be a problem if these systems are used in sensitive areas such as healthcare or criminal justice.

3 **Privacy and security:** Privacy and security are also key considerations in AI ethics. AI systems often handle sensitive personal data, and there are concerns about how this data is collected, stored and used. There are also concerns about the security of AI systems, as they may be vulnerable to hacking and other types of cyber-attacks.

4 **Human rights:** AI ethics also includes the issue of human rights, including the rights to privacy, freedom of expression and non-discrimination. There are concerns about how AI systems may impact these rights, and about the potential for AI to be used to violate human rights.

5 **Societal impact:** Another important topic in AI ethics is the issue of the societal impact of AI. This includes considerations such as the potential for AI to disrupt industries and create new job opportunities, as well as the potential for AI to exacerbate existing social and economic inequalities.

6 **Autonomy and agency:** AI systems are increasingly being developed with autonomous capabilities, and there are concerns about how these systems will make decisions and what role humans will play in the decision-making process. There are also concerns about the potential for AI systems to have agency, or the ability to act on their own behalf.

7 **Ethical frameworks and principles:** There are also ongoing debates about the ethical frameworks and principles that should be used to guide the development and use of AI. These

debates involve considerations such as the values and goals that should be prioritized in the development of AI, and the ways in which these values and goals can be operationalized and measured.

8 **Public engagement and participation:** AI ethics also involves the issue of public engagement and participation, including the need for public dialogue and consultation about the development and use of AI. There are concerns about the need for inclusive and diverse participation in these debates, and about the ways in which the public can be involved in the development of AI policies and practices.

9 **Interdisciplinary approaches:** Finally, AI ethics involves the need for interdisciplinary approaches that bring together expertise from a range of fields, including computer science, philosophy, law, sociology and other disciplines. This is important because AI has the potential to impact many different aspects of society, and there is a need for a diverse range of perspectives to be considered when developing ethical approaches to AI.

Safety

The term 'safe and trustworthy AI' is relatively new. It expands on the fundamental concepts of fairness and transparency that have been a constant guiding principle for AI ethics.

But its remit is now much larger than was originally thought. We now understand the significant impact of foundational or frontier models that quickly become embedded in so many different applications and solutions. If they are not properly tested and certified before this rapid utility, there is a major risk that underlying problems will be amplified just from widespread use.

The UK Government have led the world, organizing the first global AI Safety Summit in 2023. While the summit was small in terms of the number of attendees, it had participation from many of the world's governments and major technology players, and agreed to set up a dedicated AI safety institute.[1]

Digital trust and trustworthy AI

As part of the safety remit, how we build trust with users of these AI-based solutions, having access to our data and with the power to make life-changing decisions, is increasingly important.

We need more infrastructure in place that can help demonstrate strong data stewardship and allow users to make active decisions on how their valuable information is used, both in the training of these models but also in the act of decision making.

I believe this is going to be an area of strong innovation and future capability, creating opportunities at all levels of the AI pipeline, from start-ups to the largest corporations. New roles and career paths will emerge from this area of research – one to watch out for.

Core AI principles

Organizations will define their own core principles for how they build and use AI both internally and externally. These will be used to govern and control the entire data science process and workflow. They will also inform staff, shareholders, partners and customers on the approach any company has for this most important and disruptive technology.

As an example, below is listed a suggested set of core AI principles that could be used within any organization. These principles could be used to inform the use and application of AI across all areas and functions of a business.

For each principle we expand on the various aspects likely to be included in any detailed AI policy or AI strategy for ethics and responsible AI.

FIGURE 11.1 Example set of AI core principles

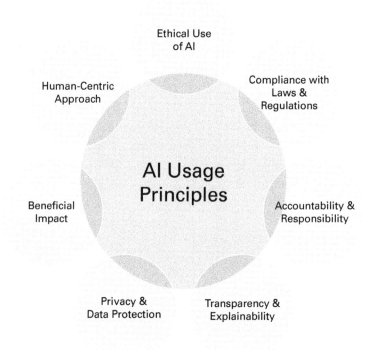

Ethical Use
of AI

Human-Centric
Approach

Compliance with
Laws &
Regulations

Beneficial
Impact

AI Usage Principles

Accountability &
Responsibility

Privacy &
Data Protection

Transparency &
Explainability

Principle One: Ethical use of AI

Obviously, AI systems have the potential to impact individuals, communities and society as a whole. As such, we need to collectively pledge to use, develop, deploy and manage AI technologies in a manner consistent with ethical principles, respect for human rights and societal values.

Ethical responsibility:
Commitment begins with the acknowledgement of ethical responsibility. Understand that AI technologies, when wielded irresponsibly, can have adverse consequences. Therefore, a

pledge to proactively address the ethical dimensions of AI throughout its lifecycle, from conception and development to deployment and maintenance, is important.

Safeguarding human rights:
Recognizing the importance of preserving and protecting human rights in the AI era is key. The approach to AI adoption should always include a rigorous assessment of potential human rights implications. This involves ensuring that AI does not infringe upon privacy, freedom of expression or any other fundamental rights.

Societal impact assessment:
An assessment on the societal impact of AI must be actioned. AI can reshape industries, create new opportunities and potentially disrupt existing norms. Therefore, it is important to undertake ongoing evaluations to anticipate and mitigate any adverse consequences of AI, particularly those that may disproportionately affect vulnerable populations.

Promoting positive change:
AI is a powerful tool for positive change, and can be employed to address pressing societal challenges, enhance quality of life and contribute to the advancement of knowledge, without sacrificing ethical considerations.

Ethical decision making:
Ethical considerations should be at the forefront of the decision-making process for any company, prioritizing responsible AI development, deployment and management by conducting thorough ethical assessments and continuously monitoring the impact of AI initiatives on individuals and society.

Principle Two: Compliance with applicable laws and regulations

Most, if not all organizations are dedicated to complying with all relevant local, national and international laws, regulations and industry standards governing the use of AI technologies.

This includes but is not limited to data protection and privacy laws (e.g. the General Data Protection Regulation (GDPR), the California Consumer Privacy Act (CCPA)), anti-discrimination regulations, intellectual property rights and any other relevant legal requirements.

Legal responsibility:
An organization's commitment to compliance begins with a deep sense of legal responsibility, acknowledging that the use of AI technologies carries inherent legal obligations and that we are unwavering in our commitment to meeting these obligations in every facet of our AI operations.

Data protection and privacy:
One critical aspect of compliance involves the stringent adherence to data protection and privacy laws, such as GDPR and the CCPA. To safeguard individuals' personal data, AI systems must adhere to the highest standards of data protection and privacy.

Anti-discrimination and fairness:
AI systems must be developed and deployed with a commitment to fairness and anti-discrimination principles. Companies should not engage in any practices that could lead to bias, discrimination or unfair treatment based on race, gender, age or any other protected characteristic. They must ensure that AI will be designed to promote diversity, equity and inclusion.

Intellectual property rights:
Respecting intellectual property rights is an integral part of corporate compliance. Companies should not infringe upon the intellectual property of others in the AI development and deployment activities, and must take necessary steps to protect their own intellectual property in the AI space.

Transparency in governance:
To ensure compliance, companies will maintain transparent governance structures across the organization. They will appoint dedicated compliance officers and legal experts to oversee AI-related activities, conduct regular audits and keep abreast of evolving legal requirements in the AI field.

Training and education:
Firms will invest in ongoing training and education for employees to ensure that they are well informed about AI-related legal requirements. This empowers them to make informed decisions and mitigate legal risks associated with AI use.

Collaboration with regulatory bodies:
Organizations will be committed to actively collaborating with regulatory bodies and industry associations to help shape responsible AI practices and standards. They will participate in discussions, share knowledge and support the development of regulatory frameworks that ensure the ethical and lawful use of AI.

Principle Three: Accountability and responsibility

Accountability and responsibility are core tenets of any AI governance regime, holding those involved accountable for the outcomes and impacts of AI systems deployed within an organization. Responsibility for AI decisions and actions is clearly defined and aligned with organizational roles and structures. Clear roles and responsibilities should be assigned to individuals and teams involved in building and using AI.

Accountability for outcomes:
Business leaders will want to hold themselves accountable for the outcomes and impacts of AI systems deployed within their organization. Whether the consequences are positive or negative, they take responsibility for the results of all AI initiatives. This commitment extends to the actions and decisions made by AI systems under our control.

Defining roles and responsibilities:
Clear roles and responsibilities are essential components of our accountability framework. Firms should ensure that individuals and teams involved in AI development, deployment and management have well-defined roles that align with the organizational structures. This clarity helps establish lines of

responsibility, making it evident who is accountable for specific aspects of AI projects.

Transparency in decision making:

Transparency is key to accountability. Companies must act to maintain transparency in all AI decision-making processes, ensuring that individuals involved in AI projects are aware of their responsibilities and the potential implications of their decisions. Open communication fosters a culture of accountability within our organization.

Ethical and legal accountability:

In addition to organizational accountability, leaders should recognize the importance of ethical and legal accountability. AI initiatives must adhere to ethical guidelines and comply with all relevant laws and regulations. Organizations should be committed to conducting AI activities in an ethical manner, aligning with corporate values and societal standards.

Continuous monitoring and evaluation:

Accountability is an ongoing process, therefore firms should continuously monitor and evaluate the performance of AI systems and the impact of their actions. This proactive approach helps to identify and address any issues promptly, ensuring that AI remains a positive force within the organization.

Responsibility for AI actions:

Organizations should take responsibility for the actions of AI systems under their control. This includes addressing any unintended consequences, bias or ethical dilemmas that may arise. They are most likely to commit to rectifying any negative outcomes and learning from these experiences to improve their AI practices.

Training and education:

It is important that companies invest in the training and education of individuals and teams to ensure that they are well equipped to fulfil their roles and responsibilities in AI projects. This includes providing them with the knowledge and tools necessary to make informed decisions and mitigate risks.

Principle Four: Transparency and explainability

Transparency and explainability are vital to building trust in the use of AI systems. Organizations of all sizes should commit to making AI processes, decisions and outcomes as transparent as possible while ensuring that individuals and stakeholders can understand and seek explanations for AI-generated results when necessary.

The importance of transparency:
Transparency is fundamental to trust. Companies must recognize that to foster trust in AI systems, they must provide visibility into how they operate. This includes making the inner workings of AI algorithms, data sources and decision-making processes accessible to individuals and stakeholders.

Accessible explanations:
Explainability goes hand in hand with transparency. Firms should commit to ensuring that individuals and stakeholders can seek explanations for AI-generated results when needed. Their AI systems must provide clear and accessible explanations that are comprehensible to non-technical users.

Empowering individuals:
A progressive view is that transparency and explainability are tools for empowerment. By providing individuals with insight into how AI decisions are made, we enable them to make informed choices and exercise agency in their interactions with AI systems.

Privacy and data transparency:
Transparency also encompasses data usage and privacy. Organizations will be committed to being transparent about the data they collect, how it is used and the measures in place to protect individuals' privacy rights. Individuals have the right to know how their data is utilized in AI systems.

Compliance with regulations:
Transparency efforts should align with legal and regulatory requirements such as GDPR's 'right to explanation', ensuring that individuals can exercise their rights to seek explanations and understand the basis of AI decisions as mandated by relevant laws.

User-friendly communication:
It will help to prioritize user-friendly communication in any transparency and explainability efforts. This includes using plain language and visual aids to make complex AI processes and outcomes more understandable to a broader audience.

Principle Five: Privacy and data protection

The privacy and protection of individuals' data are paramount. Firms must adhere to rigorous data privacy and protection standards, ensuring that personal and sensitive data used in AI systems is handled in accordance with applicable laws and regulations. This includes data anonymization, encryption and access controls.

Data privacy and legal compliance:
Commitment to data privacy and protection begins with strict adherence to applicable laws and regulations governing data privacy, such as GDPR and the CCPA. Companies will take all necessary measures to ensure that AI systems are in compliance with these legal standards.

Data minimization and anonymization:
A sensible approach is to practise data minimization, ensuring that only the data necessary for specific AI applications is collected and used, in addition to employing robust data anonymization techniques to protect individuals' identities and privacy. Data that is not necessary for AI processing is carefully excluded to minimize potential risks.

Encryption and security measures:

To safeguard personal and sensitive data, firms should implement state-of-the-art encryption and security measures, ensuring that data at rest and in transit is protected to prevent unauthorized access, breaches or data leaks. Security protocols must align with industry best practices to maintain data integrity and confidentiality.

Access controls and permissions:

Best practice is to establish stringent access controls and permissions to limit who can access and manipulate data within our AI systems. These controls are designed to prevent unauthorized access and misuse of data, further reinforcing data protection.

Ethical data handling:

Organizations should demonstrate a commitment to data privacy that extends to ethical data handling, ensuring that data used in AI systems is treated with the utmost respect and that we avoid any unethical practices, including the use of personal data for purposes other than those explicitly authorized by individuals.

Transparency in data practices:

The data teams must maintain transparency in data practices. Individuals are informed about the types of data collected, how it is used and the purposes for which it is employed in our AI systems. They should also provide individuals with clear information about their data rights and how to exercise them.

Continuous monitoring and auditing:

The IT governance department will engage in continuous monitoring and auditing of data-handling practices to ensure ongoing compliance with data privacy and protection standards. Any identified issues are promptly addressed to maintain the highest levels of data security.

Data subject rights:
Corporates are obligated to respect data subject rights, such as the right to access, rectify or delete personal data. Individuals have the right to control their data within AI systems, and firms will provide mechanisms for them to exercise these rights.

Principle Six: Beneficial impact

Companies will look to leverage AI technologies for the benefit of their stakeholders, including customers, employees, partners and the wider community. They will strive to maximize the positive impact of AI while minimizing potential harm, through improved efficiency, better decision making and enhanced user experiences. Simultaneously, they will be dedicated to minimizing any potential negative impacts or harm that may arise from AI use.

Maximizing positive impact:
A primary goal in this modern AI-driven environment is to maximize the positive impact of AI across all aspects of a firm's operations. This includes improving efficiency, enhancing decision-making processes and creating superior user experiences, viewing AI as a powerful tool to drive innovation and positive change, and actively seeking opportunities to leverage AI for the benefit of stakeholders.

User-centric approach:
A user-centric approach is likely to be central to any commitment to beneficial impact. Organizations will actively engage with customers and communities to understand their needs, preferences and concerns when it comes to AI applications. This ensures that the AI solutions developed are tailored to deliver tangible benefits and enhance the well-being of all stakeholders.

Mitigating negative impacts:
Most companies will be striving for maximum positive impact
and will be equally dedicated to minimizing and mitigating
any potential negative consequences or harm stemming from
AI use. This includes addressing issues related to bias, discrimination, privacy infringement and any other adverse effects that may arise.

Continuous improvement:
In this fast-paced environment the AI landscape is dynamic and
technology evolves rapidly. Therefore, organizations need to
be committed to continuous improvement of AI practices, actively monitoring and assessing the impact of AI deployments
and adjusting strategies to ensure that the benefits continue to
outweigh any potential harms.

Collaboration for impact:
With such a connected and networked world, firms must actively collaborate with partners, customers and the wider
community to identify opportunities for AI-driven positive
impact. By working together, we can maximize the collective
benefits that AI can bring to society.

Principle Seven: Human-centric approach

AI technologies are tools that should enhance human capabilities and augment decision making, not replace human judgment
and empathy. Prioritizing a human-centric approach in the use
of AI tools and applications allows consideration of the well-
being and needs of individuals and communities in every
AI-related decision. Everyone should recognize the importance
of human judgment, empathy and ethical considerations in any
AI use.

AI as an enhancement, not a replacement:
Central to any human-centric approach is the understanding
that AI is a tool meant to empower and augment human capabilities. View AI as a means to enhance decision making,
efficiency and productivity, but not as a substitute for the

unique qualities of human judgment, empathy and ethical discernment.

Empathy and ethical considerations:

Place a strong emphasis on the role of empathy and ethical considerations in the development and deployment of AI technologies. Acknowledge that AI systems must be designed with empathy in mind, considering the potential impact on human emotions and experiences. Furthermore, commit to integrating ethical considerations into AI decision-making processes to ensure that the technologies deployed align with these values and respect human rights.

User-centred design:

Ideally the approach to AI development follows a user-centred design philosophy. Actively engage with individuals and communities to understand their needs, preferences and concerns when it comes to AI applications. This user-centric approach ensures that AI solutions are tailored to benefit and empower the people who interact with them.

Enhancing human potential:

AI is a means to enhance human potential across various domains and functions. The aim is to develop AI applications that not only improve efficiency but also contribute positively to everyone involved, including both staff and clients.

Human oversight and control:

The importance of human oversight and control in AI systems is widely recognized and we should ensure that humans retain the ability to intervene, modify or override AI-generated decisions when necessary, especially in critical domains where human judgment is irreplaceable.

Addressing bias and fairness:

The human-centric approach extends to addressing bias and promoting fairness in AI systems. Be committed to identifying and mitigating bias in AI algorithms to ensure equitable outcomes for all individuals, regardless of their background or characteristics.

Transparency and education:
To empower individuals and communities in their interactions with AI, firms need to prioritize transparency and education. Providing clear explanations of how AI systems work, their limitations and the data they use enables users to make informed decisions and maintain control over their AI interactions.

AI governance management

The role of AI governance is to ensure all use-cases and AI developments are aligned to the core AI principles (and policies) and have followed all steps needed to ensure no regulatory, legal or other business risks from implementation occur.

In most cases AI governance is simply considered as part of the overall IT governance in that there is not a real specific need to set up separate forums/committees/review panels etc. just for AI projects/applications.

Alignment with IT governance structure

As part of the standard software development lifecycle (SDLC), much of AI governance can be integrated into already-existing forums, so it will most likely be unnecessary to form dedicated committees or meetings for the governance and risk management of introducing AI into the business and/or products and services.

For example, acceptance of use-cases and the solution approach would be reviewed in the normal IT Architectural and Design Review Committee. Then before any AI model is released, it would follow the normal SDLC workflow with quality assurance testing and release review meetings and approval.

To inform these reviews, checkpoints and tollgates, the data science workflow and process will need to document various aspects of its data privacy and ethics impact assessments together with data transparency information (what data has been used to train) and approaches used to identify and remove data bias.

AI ethics checkpoints within the data science process

The data science teams would implement various tools to help check for unintended consequences with their models, from statistical checks to surface any potential issues on data bias, to encryption techniques (such as homomorphic encryption) and other methods such as counterfactual testing. All to help minimize any risks of issues occurring once the model is put into a live environment.

During governance and release reviews, evidence of these methods would be provided to demonstrate that a thorough process of development has been followed. Essentially these are the documented answers to the questions that will be asked during the governance review of AI implementations.

Roles and responsibilities

As you look to integrate AI governance into the overall IT governance, there may be a need to assign specific roles to ensure the proper oversight and considerations are achieved.

AI ETHICS OFFICER

The role of an AI ethics officer is to ensure every implementation of AI within the organization aligns and complies with the core AI principles and wider ethical considerations detailed in this policy.

This role provides guidance to the IT and data science teams, as well as providing input into the governance decision-making process for approval of new or updated AI applications.

For smaller organizations, the scope of this role might be performed by the current risk and compliance officer.

SENIOR MANAGEMENT

The senior management are required to set the moral compass for the organization when it comes to AI ethics and governance.

By taking the topic of AI ethics seriously, it will filter down into the rest of the organization and help ensure it is given the right level of attention throughout the lifecycle of AI design, development and deployment.

Final thoughts

While this topic is immensely important and will be a key factor in the longer-term success of AI, there needs to be balance. We are still, in many ways, at the early stages of AI innovation and we need to provide some degree of freedom to allow researchers and companies to explore the art of the possible.

We already see that countries are positioning themselves at different points of this scale, and this may change the global dynamics of where AI is built and controlled. After all, the mastery of AI is the current race for global dominance.

However, there needs to be balance, and we must not sacrifice best practice development of technology because of the pressures of innovation and commercial success. Many believe we only have one opportunity to get it right with AI and so the correct level of oversight, control, audit and governance, with emphasis on ethical and responsible application, will be essential for the long-term benefits AI can deliver.

Note

1 Chair's Summary of the AI Safety Summit 2023, Bletchley Park, www.gov.uk/government/publications/aisafety-summit-2023-chairs-statement-2-november/chairs-summary-of-the-ai-safety-summit-2023-bletchley-park (archived at https://perma.cc/2WWF-75D8)

PART FOUR

The people

People are the key to all technology advancement and change; without us nothing really happens. However, we are entering a new phase that brings AI-powered technology to augment the abilities of us all regardless of our role. Even the profession of data science will be dramatically enhanced with AI agents to help us build predictive models, optimize their configuration and performance and even help with their deployment, monitoring and maintenance.

With technology building technology, people will need to do more creative and complex work, looking at the bigger-picture issues and solving the most challenging problems that even AI isn't yet ready to solve.

The demand for AI talent is large and growing rapidly at the moment, which means there is plenty of opportunity for those who want to move into this field. But we also need people with a variety of skills and abilities; it's not just about those who can build the tech, we need a range of roles that cover the full lifecycle and many disciplines. The opportunities are far and wide to work with or in AI. Now is your chance to work with the most interesting and impactful technology, at a time that we are seeing an exponential rate of change. Exciting times for all involved.

CHAPTER TWELVE

People: key characteristics

People are unique, with such a diversity of skills, experience, knowledge and abilities. Building teams of people who have complementary skills and experience will be vital to the success of any IT department building AI capabilities. Typically, anyone working in the field of AI will need a combination of some technical skills as well as the soft skills.

In terms of the soft skills, effective communication is paramount, as data scientists must convey their findings and insights to both technical and non-technical stakeholders. Problem-solving skills are also critical, as data scientists are often tasked with unravelling complex issues and devising innovative solutions. A deep curiosity to explore and understand data is vital, as is the ability to think critically and approach problems with a creative mindset. Adaptability is another key soft skill, given the rapidly evolving nature of data science and the need to stay updated with emerging techniques and technologies. Lastly, a strong sense of ethics and responsibility is essential, as data scientists often handle sensitive and confidential information, necessitating a commitment to data privacy and ethical data practices.

Key characteristics of a data scientist

So, what makes a good data scientist? Well, there are several key characteristics and traits that are important:

1 **Strong analytical skills:** Data scientists need to be able to analyse and interpret complex data, and to draw meaningful conclusions from it.
2 **Strong problem-solving skills:** Data scientists are often faced with complex problems that require creative and innovative solutions.
3 **Strong communication skills:** Data scientists need to be able to communicate their findings and recommendations effectively to a wide range of audiences, both technical and non-technical.
4 **Strong teamwork skills:** Data science projects often involve working with a team of other data scientists, as well as subject matter experts and stakeholders.

To develop and maintain these skills and traits, it is important for data scientists to continuously learn and stay up to date with new tools and techniques, and to seek out opportunities to practise and apply their skills through projects and real-world experience.

It is also very important for data scientists to understand the business area and industry. Ultimately the data will be a real-world and real-time reflection of what is happening with the business. It is important to be informed on both short-term and long-term objectives and priorities of the business.

Problem solving

Problem-solving skills are at the core of a data scientist's role, as they are tasked with tackling complex and often ambiguous data-related challenges. Firstly, data scientists must excel in defining problems clearly and precisely. This involves breaking down intricate issues into manageable components, identifying the key variables and formulating well-defined research questions. The ability to frame problems effectively sets the foundation for devising appropriate data-driven solutions.

Secondly, data scientists must exhibit strong analytical skills. They need to choose the right statistical and machine learning techniques to apply to a given problem, effectively handling and processing large datasets and identifying meaningful patterns, trends or anomalies within the data. Proficiency in data visualization is also crucial, as it enables data scientists to convey their findings visually, making complex information more accessible and aiding in problem solving for both technical and non-technical stakeholders.

Data scientists must be proficient at developing innovative approaches to problem solving. This includes the capacity to think outside the box, explore unconventional solutions and adapt to changing circumstances or new data. Creativity is key when addressing unique or unforeseen challenges that may arise in the realm of data science. Moreover, a strong foundation in domain knowledge and the ability to draw connections between data-driven insights and real-world applications are instrumental in delivering effective problem-solving outcomes as a data scientist.

Communication skills

Effective communication skills are essential for data scientists in today's data-driven world. First and foremost, data scientists must be proficient in translating complex technical findings and insights into clear and understandable language for non-technical stakeholders. This ability to bridge the gap between technical and non-technical teams is crucial in ensuring that data-driven recommendations and insights can be readily acted upon by decision makers across the organization. Clarity, simplicity and the use of visual aids like charts and graphs are indispensable tools for conveying complex data concepts effectively.

Furthermore, data scientists must possess strong interpersonal skills to collaborate effectively within cross-functional teams. Collaborative communication involves active listening, empathy and the ability to articulate data-related concepts in a way that fosters mutual understanding among team members. Data scientists often work alongside engineers, business analysts and domain experts, so the capacity to engage in productive discussions, ask insightful questions and integrate diverse perspectives is invaluable in solving complex problems and driving data-driven decision making.

Another key aspect is that data scientists must be skilled at presenting their findings persuasively. This entails constructing compelling narratives around data-driven insights and tailoring presentations to the specific needs and preferences of the audience. Whether speaking to C-suite executives, technical teams or external stakeholders, data scientists must convey the significance of their findings, the implications for the organization and the recommended actions clearly and convincingly. Effective communication not only facilitates informed decision making but also enhances the impact and influence of data scientists within their organizations.

Teamwork, office politics and personalities

Office politics and clashing personalities can often have an impact on your career progress, either within a corporate environment or in a start-up company. Identifying these potential issues as soon as possible and developing strategies to navigate them will be another key success factor.

These potential issues can be very time consuming and stressful for the individuals involved. It is likely that during the course of your career you will experience this yourself or know someone else who has or is currently.

You will likely experience people who are more vocal, taking credit for your contributions and work efforts or not pulling their weight on team assignments, constantly finding excuses or reasons why they can't do something, blaming other people or situations that have impacted them.

These types of issues are always frustrating, and normally, while annoying, tend to resolve themselves over time, as the manager will spot the recurring problems and will need to act to help the individual change their approach.

However, sometimes a leopard doesn't change their spots, and some individuals have deep-rooted personality traits that mean this type of behaviour seems to be genetically programmed into how they work. It is well documented that certain personalities can have a disruptive impact on the workplace and workforce. If you find yourself subjected to this ongoing problem, then you may need to be more proactive to reduce the impact on yourself.

These issues are common in any workplace, and any size of organization and industry. Certainly, this is not unique to a career in AI. However, throughout my career in technology, I have come across my fair share of difficult personalities that required careful management and consideration to overcome, reducing their effect on my own career path.

Community support

The world of AI has always had a sharing and open culture, although this is slightly changing now due to the commercial and competitive environment as AI gains more utility. However, the fundamental principles of sharing and learning are still very much at the core of our industry. There is a vast amount of open and free information available for anyone who wants to educate themselves and increase their understanding of the subject.

There are community networks, groups, clubs and events that provide wonderful opportunities for everyone to engage with the fast-moving technology.

This community-based sharing must continue as we build on the capabilities and deliver increasingly complex solutions. Open innovation and invention will be the best way for us to ensure responsible and trustworthy AI is built and utilized widely in all corners of the world. Only a community and open approach will allow us to make data science a profession to be proud about, with everyone involved looking to follow best practice to deliver robust and reliable solutions.

Final thoughts

Most of us will spend the majority of our time and life in a working environment. Working with a vast array of people, some will become our best friends, others we will frequently clash with on a professional level, maybe one or two we simply cannot work with.

Ultimately the workplace needs a diversity of people, ideas, approaches and capabilities; we all need to respect each other, as we are all on a journey of learning and no one is perfect. One of the most beautiful experiences in life is when you help others, and in return, when you need help you will find it too. Without getting religious, there is karma in this world.

Sometimes, with my own career, changes have happened, been imposed on me, that at the time I was very unhappy about. But on reflection, when I look back with a more balanced perspective, I can see that it was totally the right decision and the best thing for me – sometimes you have to trust the people around you to know this sooner than you know it yourself.

Your working life will have ups and downs, and sometimes it can be difficult, uncomfortable even. When this has happened to me, I tell myself to give it time (six months), as often things will change again, get better, or I will realize I am benefiting from the change.

Many times when the workplace is more challenging than normal, or a particular project is exceptionally fraught with issues (red projects), this is when you as an individual will learn much more. It's the challenging and difficult projects or work we always remember best, on reflection having learnt the most from them.

Your career is unique to you; it will provide you with much opportunity and will enrich your life in so many different ways. Learning and mastering AI is going to be a significant part of your career story now – it is a huge opportunity, so run with it.

CHAPTER THIRTEEN

Different teams and roles

E very company and IT department will be slightly different in
the way they decide to organize teams and work together.
Every head of development, data science and CTO will have
strong opinions on the right way to do things. There is no right
or wrong but it's more about what is considered best practice
and how to best align with the rest of the organization.

It will also very much depend on the maturity of AI adoption,
based on the 10 stages or three phases as illustrated in the AI
adoption journey diagram in Chapter 3, and the spread of AI
across the organization too. The size of the organization and the
way it is internally organized will also influence these structure
decisions.

In this chapter I will highlight how all the various roles fit
together to form a team or teams that can effectively and efficiently perform as required.

Data science pods

Development methodologies have changed over the years; while Waterfall was the de facto approach years ago, most teams and project/programme management have moved to one form of Agile development, taking a more incremental approach. The Agile approach requires small teams that can develop complete tasks, front to back, from the database changes to the user interface and everything in between, which in our situation includes the AI and ML models. These teams are typically referred to as pods (or sprint teams), and the make-up of the individuals and roles within them can be dependent on many factors.

Data science pods may be considered to be a specialist type of Agile development team that has data science members to support the activity of building and integrating ML models into the specific build tasks.

The size of a pod can also vary, from three or four people up to seven or eight. Sometimes an individual might have more than one role in the pod. Pod structures can also change over time, adding more people as the recruitment process finds additional resources.

Pod roles

For data science pods, there are some essential, core roles that are needed as well as some optional supporting roles:

Data engineer: Data engineers are responsible for designing and building the infrastructure and processes for storing, processing and analysing data. They work on tasks such as building data pipelines, extract, transform and load (ETL) processes, and data storage and management systems.

Machine learning engineer: Machine learning engineers are responsible for designing, building and deploying machine learning models and systems. They work on tasks such as developing and training machine learning models and integrating them into production environments.

Business intelligence analyst: Business intelligence analysts are responsible for collecting, analysing and reporting on business data. They work on tasks such as building dashboards, creating reports and providing insights to decision makers.

Data analyst: Data analysts are responsible for collecting, cleaning and analysing data. They work on tasks such as identifying trends and patterns in data, and creating reports and visualizations to communicate their findings.

Software developer: Software developers are responsible for designing and building software applications. They work on tasks such as writing code, testing and debugging applications, and maintaining and updating software. Those who can work on all parts of the technology stack, from database to front-end, are sometimes referred to as full-stack developers.

Product owner: Often a business user who essentially is the client of the application or system being built, they will have a view on relative priorities of functionality as well as giving clarity on how specific parts of the application should operate.

Sprint master: Runs the sprint meetings and overall helps to eliminate any impediments and blockers that other team members face, ensuring the smooth running of the sprint team.

Supporting roles

DevOps or MLOps engineer: DevOps engineers are responsible for the integration and delivery of software applications. They work on tasks such as automating the build, test and deployment processes, and maintaining the infrastructure and tools used for software development. This role might be shared across several pods, or sit external to the pods but be leveraged as an additional part-resource as needed.

Data visualization: Often there will be a need to showcase the predictive insights from the ML models; a specialist to visualize these outcomes helps to make the data narrative easy to consume and explain.

User experience (UX) designer: Depending on the application solution there may be a need to design the user interface to align with the data analytics and potential user feedback needed.

As the field develops in the coming years, there will be new roles created that simply don't exist at the moment.

Other roles (outside of the pods)

There will be many other potential roles needed that will sit outside of the individual pods but support the group/pod teams. Some of these roles may still have day-to-day involvement, while others may only be consulted from time to time as needed:

Data ethics officer: A data ethics officer is responsible for ensuring that an organization's data practices are ethical and responsible. This can include tasks such as developing and implementing data ethics policies, conducting risk assessments and advising on ethical issues related to data.

Data bias mitigation specialist: A data bias mitigation specialist is responsible for identifying and addressing biases in data and data-driven systems. This can include tasks such as analysing data for bias, developing strategies for mitigating bias and conducting evaluations of the fairness and bias of data-driven systems.

Systems administrator: Systems administrators are responsible for the maintenance, operation and security of computer systems.

They work on tasks such as installing and configuring systems, managing user accounts and troubleshooting issues.

Data architect: Data architects are responsible for designing and managing the data infrastructure of an organization. They work on tasks such as defining data models, selecting data storage technologies and implementing data security and privacy measures.

Cloud solutions architect: Cloud solutions architects are responsible for designing and implementing cloud-based systems and solutions. They work on tasks such as selecting cloud platforms and technologies, and designing and implementing cloud-based applications and infrastructure.

Information security analyst: Information security analysts are responsible for protecting an organization's computer systems and networks from cyber threats. They work on tasks such as identifying and addressing security vulnerabilities and implementing security measures and policies.

Data governance manager: A data governance manager is responsible for establishing and maintaining the policies and processes for managing and protecting an organization's data assets. This can include tasks such as defining data ownership and access rights, establishing data security and privacy policies and implementing data governance frameworks.

Data compliance officer: A data compliance officer is responsible for ensuring that an organization's data practices are compliant with relevant laws and regulations. This can include tasks such as conducting risk assessments, developing and implementing compliance policies and advising on compliance issues related to data.

Other stakeholders

Any IT department will have a range of stakeholders that have a vested interest in the success of different projects.

Obviously, you have the head of the business area (business users) that the application/functionality is being built for. They will be very keen to check the ML models are working as anticipated in all situations.

Aligned to that you will have the head of the IT team or group that is responsible for directly supporting that business team/function.

You will also have other IT roles as stakeholders, including architecture, risk and compliance, internal audit, support teams and the testing teams. More senior IT roles may also have visibility or direct influence depending on the scale of the project, including the CAIO, CTO, CIO, CDO and maybe even the CEO of the country or region (depending on the size of the firm).

Understanding the specific corporate landscape and range of potential stakeholders that need to be engaged with at particular times in the project is essential for a smooth delivery.

Communities of practice

With large organizations, it is important to engage with the entire firm, collaborating and sharing learnings with everyone, ensuring all have the opportunity to get involved and contribute to the early stages of AI utilization. It is important that everyone across the organization feels they have a voice in the way AI is deployed and a role to play in the initial approach to AI integration.

Setting up a community of practice (CoP), working group or steering committee can be the best way to initially socialize the early stages of introduction of AI. Here the CoP can help define the best practices, standards, tools and frameworks to be used across the firm or group. This allows people to have some control in how AI is implemented within their own area, helping to facilitate a smoother integration.

CASE STUDY The Machine Learning Working Group at Credit Suisse

Back in 2016 I was working at Credit Suisse within the Risk and Finance IT department. I could see the investment banks were starting to get interested in the use of AI and ML. I realized the importance of coordinating efforts across the different groups within the firm, both technology teams and business users. I therefore set up the Machine Learning Working Group (MLWG) as a virtual team, connecting everyone across the company who was interested in or developing ML pilots or proofs of concept. Quick to establish, we had over 100 members across the entire firm contributing to efforts to define a strategy, standards and best practices, and share experiences, code and insights. We invited AI vendors to present their technology to us to review, and worked with senior architects and management to get everyone who should be a stakeholder involved with the group. It was a huge success and it continued to operate long after I left the firm. It helped to shape the AI strategy for Credit Suisse, and coordinate efforts across groups who would not normally collaborate. This group set the groundwork for the data science centre of excellence, which was formed afterwards and took much of what we had produced as a foundation to work with.

Organizational structure

For small firms, this might seem trivial, but for larger organizations, the way data science teams are set up, with supporting teams and groups too, can be an important factor for success and is an important element of any AI strategy (as defined in Chapter 9 on AI strategy).

As previously mentioned, the organizational structure of data science teams depends on many factors including the size of the organization and the maturity of AI adoption (yes, the structure is likely to change over time as the experience with AI across the firm grows).

Final thoughts

Knowing how a company organizes itself and your place within it is a good start to determine how you will navigate your way towards promotion and increased responsibility (if that is what you are looking for). Some firms expect you to want to advance yourself and rise through the levels of job roles and responsibilities, while others are happy as long as you are performing well.

Many companies will have times when they reorganize themselves, for various reasons, and these times can be additional opportunities for career changes and advancement. Keeping your finger on the pulse of what is happening can give you an early warning of these potential openings.

CHAPTER FOURTEEN

Getting started

Getting started on a new career path is often the most diffi-cult part of any career. It will depend on your own personal situation and prior background as to the best way to get started. In this chapter we provide advice and guidance on the different approaches you might take but ultimately everyone is unique and will therefore tread a different path from others. There is no right or wrong answer here. Reflecting on my own career demonstrates this very point. My journey, experience and knowledge, gained with the various roles and companies I have worked for, creates a unique resumé that will be perfect for some future roles and less so for others. We each have to navigate and carve out our own specific career path, with each step along the way being the best next step along the way to our future.

This is both exciting and terrifying at the same time. I know, from mentoring many people in the past, the pressure of making the best first step. For those looking to make a dramatic change in direction, it can be tough to highlight the relevant experience and skills for a new challenge to give yourself the best possible opportunity.

In both circumstances, one needs to find ways to stand out from the crowd, as while there is high demand for AI practitioners, there is also much competition – and if you are new to the field, you need to demonstrate the desire and enthusiasm you have for the technology (and the application industry). Don't forget, it's your background, interests, passions, experience and knowledge that make you unique and potentially perfect for some roles, and you may not really know what the hiring manager is actually looking for from a job description.

I will divide the advice based on your time in the commercial workforce, either as a student looking for their first job, or a professional looking for a change in direction.

Students and first job

If you are interested in becoming a data scientist, there are several steps you can take to start learning and building your skills:

1 **Build a strong foundation in mathematics and statistics:** This includes topics like linear algebra, calculus, probability and statistical inference.
2 **Learn a programming language:** Data scientists typically use languages like Python or R for data manipulation, visualization and machine learning.
3 **Explore online resources:** There are many online courses, textbooks and tutorials available for learning data science. Some popular options include Coursera, edX and DataCamp.
4 **Practise by working on projects:** Applying your knowledge to real-world data science problems is a great way to learn and build your skills. Consider finding a dataset and working on a project that interests you.

There are many career options available for data scientists, including roles in industry, academia, government and consulting. Some common job titles for data scientists include data scientist, data analyst and business intelligence analyst.

To land a job as a data scientist, it is important to have a strong portfolio of projects and experience. This can include data science courses and certifications, as well as projects that you have completed on your own or as part of a team.

It is also important to have a solid understanding of the tools and techniques used in data science, and to be able to communicate your findings effectively.

Often getting your first data science role will be the most difficult, as you need to demonstrate your interest and capabilities with limited opportunities to showcase them. Doing online courses and contributing to other projects will help you illustrate your commitment to this profession.

It is also worth noting that you don't need to have a degree in computer science or machine learning to work in the IT department or data science team. It obviously helps, but it isn't essential. I know many people working in various roles in IT departments in small and large companies that don't even have STEM-based degrees. The most important success factor is to demonstrate a passion and deep desire to work in the role you are applying for. Understand the company, understand the industry and understand what the role involves.

Another consideration is that once you land your firm role as a data scientist and build up a successful track record of delivery, depending on the size of the company, you might be able to move teams and roles and try different things. Widening your experience is a wise objective in the early years of your career.

Professionals and career change

Much of the advice for students looking for their first job in AI can apply to those more mature and experienced working professionals looking to pivot into the world of AI.

The main difference is that you have much more experience in the workplace and better understand what is important and needed for specific roles. Often you can reshape the experience you have and make it relevant for this new area and industry.

While the field of AI might feel somewhat mysterious and special, it's just a piece of technology. It is more advanced and capable than much of the technology that has come before it, built differently than previous types of applications and has some unique governance and audit requirements, but apart from that it is just another bit of technology that is being used to help solve a problem.

This technology, probably more than any other, needs people to help manage and control its use; people with broad knowledge and experience, who can see potential problems before they happen, who can understand the dynamics of teams and groups interacting together, who know the value of properly testing and reviewing these types of systems. We need maturity and experience to make sure AI technology is implemented correctly, and all stakeholders are involved in every step of the development so there are no surprises on go-live.

The risks of AI-based systems going wrong and creating monumental issues means that we need mature thinking to provide the checks and balances, the tollgates and checkpoints to ensure everything is done responsibly and trustworthily. This is so important right now, and will only be more so as the adoption of AI continues to grow over the coming years.

We need much more than just academically achieving research-focused data scientists; the industry needs experience and knowledge for so many different areas. Opportunities for experienced professionals to move into the field of AI are now greater than ever before.

But the job market is competitive, so as an experienced professional looking to move into this sector, finding ways to learn as much as possible to get better informed and more knowledgeable will increase your chances and demonstrate your deep interest in the topic (you've already made a great start by reading this book!). There is a huge amount of information shared online about AI, both technical and more business focused, to allow you to become more informed about the technology. Many courses and educational resources are available too (a lot for free).

You will not need to be an expert on AI to work in AI, just to demonstrate a strong foundational understanding and an appreciation of the challenges and risks with the technology together with the opportunities and benefits. As previously detailed, there are many different roles within the AI industry, each having a varying level of technical knowledge requirements.

Other considerations

For experienced professionals, in many cases you probably will not need to move companies to start working with or in AI. Many companies will start to look to adopt AI in the coming few years (if they haven't already started). This opens opportunities for you to just align with these innovation projects and let your managers know you have a deep interest in supporting such work. Talk to your managers and other people you know across the organization; someone, somewhere will be thinking about or even starting to explore the use of AI. Find a way to get involved, supporting the initiative and providing help and guidance to those already starting to use the technology.

Adoption can come in different forms; in some cases it might be using some of the new tools and applications available, in others it might be to use new AI-based functionality available in the software products your company already uses. In other cases there might be a need to build something more customized and tailored to a specific requirement. In all of these options, there will be ways you can find to get involved and support the project to give you some initial experience.

Final thoughts

Anything you can do that demonstrates your interest and determination to move into the field of AI will be well received by any hiring manager. The subject of AI requires continuous learning, so illustrating your ability to do this anyway is a big tick for you when compared to others.

Persistence is also key to success; it is possible you won't get the first job you apply for and interview at. But it is not always just about technical abilities and skills; communication and personality fit are also factors in the hiring process. Different hiring managers will have varying priorities and risk profiles. It's a numbers game and you have to keep trying.

If you are finding the move challenging, look for companies that are working with AI and take a role closer to your own experience; then you can look to make a sideways transition after a period of time to a role that is better aligned to your longer-term objectives.

And finally, leverage the power of your network and talk to people, let them know what you are looking for – you will be amazed at what opportunities might surface for you.

No career change is easy, even one that is a similar role to the one you have been doing for a while. But there is nothing better than doing a role you want, that both challenges and excites you in equal measure.

CHAPTER FIFTEEN

Career development

Getting started with your career in AI is easier now than ever before, due to the unprecedented demand and growth in the industry but also the significant amount of information and educational training available. There will be many ways to move into the world of AI, as there is such a diversity of career opportunities and roles available.

As with any career path, you should obviously align your selection with your interests, passions, skills and goals. Finding your passion and aligning to that is probably the most important career advice you will ever get.

If you are already in the workplace, the easiest way to move towards AI could be an internal transfer to a different team that is already focused on AI adoption. Often with this type of move there is more understanding and flexibility with your level of knowledge and skills, with more focus on on-the-job learning. Often this starts by letting your manager know you have a deep interest in working with AI.

Regardless of the stage of your career and your specific skills, knowledge and experience, given the range of roles in AI and the massive adoption across many industries, there are certainly a few options available to everyone to move towards a career in AI.

One of my previous managers once told me that 80 per cent of doing a role is getting it in the first place, and in many ways he was right. Demonstrating your passion and interest in the topic will be key to unlocking your future AI career.

The AI career landscape

Let us first examine the AI landscape and understand the full range of options and opportunities available.

If you are more research inclined, then studying or working at a university would be the most obvious option; however, there are AI institutions focused on different topics (for example AI ethics) or more general ones like the Alan Turing Institute.

Some of the large tech firms, such as Google, Microsoft and Meta, have large research and applied AI departments that have thousands of people working on AI.

Many of the larger consultancy firms have large teams of data scientists (and related roles) to work on client assignments. Some of them will also invest in limited research and discovery to ensure they have sight of any of the latest changes in the technology. For example, in 2023 Accenture announced a $3 billion investment[1] to focus on generative AI.

While a lot of the above have been available as career options for many years, the following opportunities have really exploded over the last 12–18 months.

Many of the very large corporations will have been running various innovation and pilot programmes to explore the use of AI for many years. Some will have already scaled up their use of the technology in some divisions of the business. If you already work in a large corporation, while there may not be opportunities in your particular group or team, there will most likely be other groups who are more advanced with the adoption of AI, and so an internal move to a team that is working with AI might be the best first move for you to start your own focus on AI.

Businesses of all sizes, but particularly small to medium-sized enterprises (SMEs), are seriously looking at how they can benefit from the use of AI. These sizes of companies have the need, and some level of investment available, but what they really lack in many cases are the knowledgeable people to help them explore the potential of AI and guide them along the journey. CEOs, their board members and senior management are urgently investigating how AI will both impact and improve their business. If you already work in such a firm, it's time to stand up and let folks know you have an interest in helping with this AI adoption journey.

Software vendors who have established products and services but now need to include AI functionality within their offering are now also looking to build out various ML models to provide AI-driven capabilities to their clients.

The start-up ecosystem has rapidly expanded. There are pure-play AI start-ups, that is to say, start-ups that are developing something unique and novel as a general tool, framework, platform or application that can be used by many clients in different industries. There are also AI start-ups that are more applied in nature, using off-the-shelf AI techniques but applying them to new datasets and problems. The third type of start-up is actually any other type of start-up that is now realizing that it needs to integrate some AI-based functionality into its own offering.

Hopefully this shows you the depth of the AI landscape, with opportunities all around you waiting to be discovered. One of my own mentors once told me that you have to be proactive and manage your own career; you cannot just sit back and expect others to do it for you. The options are there, you just have to decide which one is right for you and go for it.

Understanding AI career paths

Ultimately everyone's career path is unique, based on the opportunities available at each step and the decisions you make. This uniqueness is what makes us all special and brings such diversity and experience to the table at the middle and later phases of your career.

Having said that, there are some obvious career paths that naturally flow from one role and responsibility to the next. These steps can be easier to achieve, as they are well trodden by many and it's simply the next stage of progression. There is nothing wrong with this, and in many cases it will be the best next step to follow. For example, if you do decide to become a data scientist, there is a range of titles and levels of roles and responsibilities, from junior to senior, lead and eventually head. This path may then lead you to even more senior roles such as CTO, CIO or CAIO. Many career paths will split into two streams. One is focused on continued technical expertise, generally referred to as an IC (individual contributor), but the specific titles will align with the technical career track as defined by the company you are working for. The other stream often aligns with managing teams and projects and is seen as a more managerial track.

Sometimes you can be promoted into a role that requires you to follow one of these two streams; you need to make sure you are comfortable with this, but sometimes it can be difficult to know until you try.

Occasionally throughout your career there will be a fork in the road, a choice to make that might change your life forever. Often one will be an easy way, with the other more challenging and potentially difficult (but likely to be both more rewarding and a better platform to learn and expand yourself).

As I look back on my career, I understand that the road is winding, with several changes along the way, some major, others minor. What is fascinating is that while one particular job had its part to play, it isn't as important as the direction of travel and the longer-term goals you have for yourself. Personally, I could not have predicted where I am right now, nor what the future might hold, but I do know it's an exciting time and anything is possible. It certainly is a wonderful time to be working in technology and specifically the field of artificial intelligence, so why not join me?

AI career options

There are a wide range of roles and opportunities within technology departments in firms. Many roles support the overall function of building intelligent systems and applications. Some of these different roles include:

Data engineer: Data engineers are responsible for designing and building the infrastructure and processes for storing, processing and analysing data. They work on tasks such as building data pipelines, extract, transform and load (ETL) processes and data storage and management systems.

Machine learning engineer: Machine learning engineers are responsible for designing, building and deploying machine learning models and systems. They work on tasks such as developing and training machine learning models and integrating them into production environments.

Business intelligence analyst: Business intelligence analysts are responsible for collecting, analysing, and reporting on business data. They work on tasks such as building dashboards, creating reports and providing insights to decision makers.

DevOps or MLOps engineer: DevOps engineers are responsible for the integration and delivery of software applications. They work on tasks such as automating the build, test and deployment process, and maintaining the infrastructure and tools used for software development.

Systems administrator: Systems administrators are responsible for the maintenance, operation and security of computer systems. They work on tasks such as installing and configuring systems, managing user accounts and troubleshooting issues.

Data analyst: Data analysts are responsible for collecting, cleaning and analysing data. They work on tasks such as identifying trends and patterns in data and creating reports and visualizations to communicate their findings.

Data architect: Data architects are responsible for designing and managing the data infrastructure of an organization. They work on tasks such as defining data models, selecting data storage technologies and implementing data security and privacy measures.

Cloud solutions architect: Cloud solutions architects are responsible for designing and implementing cloud-based systems and solutions. They work on tasks such as selecting cloud platforms and technologies and designing and implementing cloud-based applications and infrastructure.

Information security analyst: Information security analysts are responsible for protecting an organization's computer systems and networks from cyber threats. They work on tasks such as identifying and addressing security vulnerabilities and implementing security measures and policies.

Software developer: Software developers are responsible for designing and building software applications. They work on tasks such as writing code, testing and debugging applications and maintaining and updating software.

Data ethics officer: A data ethics officer is responsible for ensuring that an organization's data practices are ethical and responsible. This can include tasks such as developing and implementing data ethics policies, conducting risk assessments and advising on ethical issues related to data.

Data bias mitigation specialist: A data bias mitigation specialist is responsible for identifying and addressing biases in data and data-driven systems. This can include tasks such as analysing data for bias, developing strategies for mitigating bias and conducting evaluations of the fairness and bias of data-driven systems.

Data governance manager: A data governance manager is responsible for establishing and maintaining the policies and processes for managing and protecting an organization's data assets. This can include tasks such as defining data ownership and access rights, establishing data security and privacy policies and implementing data governance frameworks.

Data compliance officer: A data compliance officer is responsible for ensuring that an organization's data practices are compliant with relevant laws and regulations. This can include tasks such as conducting risk assessments, developing and implementing compliance policies and advising on compliance issues related to data.

As the field develops in the coming years, there will be many new roles created that simply don't exist at the moment. We have seen this happen most recently with the role of prompt engineer, and with other examples such as AI ethics officer.

Building a strong foundation

To be a successful data scientist, it is important to have a strong foundation in mathematics, statistics and computer science, as well as domain-specific knowledge and skills. Data scientists should also have strong problem-solving and communication skills and be able to work effectively in a team.

While the mathematical, analytical and computer science skills are very important, the communication skills are an essential part of the role too. While data visualization helps with this, being able to create the right narrative with the business implications of what the insights and model results are showing is a primary aspect of the data science role.

The role of data scientist is truly multi-disciplined, requiring a wide range of hard and soft skills to perform it well. This is why I am an advocate of data scientists having a broad foundation of knowledge and experience – this makes individuals who come from different areas and have various prior experiences strong candidates, but this is not mandatory.

Gaining practical experience

Ultimately, there is no substitute for hands-on experience and practical knowledge of actually how to work with AI. Anything you can do to give yourself some level of real-world practical experience will significantly help your chances of working in the field.

There are several very useful resources available to give you the chance to develop your practice skills; both Kaggle[2] and Hugging Face[3] are excellent sources of data and code to learn from.

Getting accounts with one or more of the cloud platforms and using some of the free pre-trained models is a wonderful and easy way to get started and build some confidence.

'Learn by doing' is a great motto for what you need to do. I used to take entire weeks off work (I called them my Geek Weeks) to 'sharpen the sword' of my skills and knowledge, trying new tech and learning new things. It's wonderfully refreshing for both the mind and soul.

Do a bit each day and you will be amazed by how much you can achieve in this incremental way over a few weeks and months. You simply won't recognize yourself six months or a year from now.

If you have time, volunteer to help a small organization, charity or start-up. They will be so grateful for the help, and you will gain real-world hands-on experience.

If you are a student, finding an internship with a company using or developing AI would be a great addition to your resume.

If you cannot find any work experience opportunities, just working on a personal project will give you the opportunity to learn and experiment with the technologies.

Networking and mentorship

One of the most important aspects of my career has been to find good mentors. They are an invaluable source of experience, knowledge and connections that will have such a positive impact on your working life. I have had many mentors myself over the years, and it is likely you will need to change mentor from time to time; as you grow, your needs change and therefore the experience you need from a mentor will also evolve. Eventually you will give back to the world, and be a mentor for the next generations; it's a beautiful thing to do, both as a mentor and as a mentee. Well worth the effort. To find a mentor, look for someone you aspire to be in the next three to five years, and then simply ask them. This isn't for everyone, so don't be offended if when you ask someone they turn you down – just keep looking and ask someone else.

Regardless of having a mentor or not, one of your biggest assets over your working life will be your network. Nurture and cherish it, help it grow. Value it and give to it, as well as asking for help from it. It will often surprise you in so many ways. The power of the network should not be underestimated. You will also be astonished by how people from your past can dramatically impact your future. Your network is your friend, it can help you when you most need it.

It takes time and effort to build this network in the early stages of your career, and it might feel like a complete waste of time at the beginning as you don't see any rewards or output early on. You need to stick with it, as there is a compounding benefit and essentially a need to get to a critical mass of connections. But once you get to that level, the benefits will surface when you need them.

Ultimately you will be surprised and pleased with the random opportunities a strong and wide network will offer you over time.

Staying informed and adapting

Many think that technology is now advancing at an exponential rate. From what I have seen over the last couple of years, for AI it feels like it's even faster than that. When OpenAI's ChatGPT service gained 100 million users in just two months, it changed the game not only for the AI and tech industry, but also for businesses in general. Everyone is now interested in AI and how it might change the future of work for all of us.

What this means for anyone working in the AI industry, regardless of role, is that it is increasingly challenging to keep up with the latest advances. Previously a noteworthy research paper or technique was released once every few months; now the time horizon is reduced to weeks or even days. New applications, models, research, tools and frameworks are coming out all the time. Even professors of AI are having to keep active on social media to keep well informed.

And the technology is only part of the change; new regulations, ethical concerns, AI safety summits, legal changes for AI patents and more are happening all the time too.

It's a global race and therefore exceptionally fast moving; errors are being made but the benefits outweigh the risks at this stage. AI is the new gold, and it's driving a huge rush for the prime land and opportunity.

For anyone working in AI, this now means we need to invest more time and effort into keeping up to date with all the new capabilities. A list of resources to help you with this task is available on the *Confident AI* webpage (see the bonus link for readers page at the start of this book for the details).

Landing your first AI job

This will likely be the most difficult role to get, as once you are working in the field of AI it will be a lot easier to move roles within it. In order to get started, you might have to take a less senior role than you would ideally like, or in an industry or for a company that might not be your first choice. Sometimes you might need to sacrifice a perfect role to just make a move and simply consider it a stepping-stone role.

Getting started in AI is the most important factor initially, and for some people, you may not really know what the perfect role and industry for you is yet. Sometimes you have try different things to be able to properly determine if it's a role for you. Opportunities will surface to allow you to move to different areas or roles over time, allowing you to explore different career options.

Moving around is not a bad thing; this broad experience can serve you well later in your career, as having an understanding of different roles and areas will allow you to understand how all these different aspects come together to produce an efficient and effective team.

If you are a student, getting an internship to build your portfolio of real-world experience is the perfect stepping-stone move and it will allow you to explore options before making any major decisions.

You will need to showcase your passion for the field within your resume, highlighting any training and courses you have achieved; any skills you have acquired including languages, frameworks and tools used; any books read, conferences or events attended. Demonstrate your interest and your focus on continuous learning.

Career advancement and growth

Once you have landed a job as a data scientist, there are several ways to advance in your career over time (listed below). But ultimately, you need to keep your ear to the ground and get a sense of any new role opportunities before others do, as this is always a competitive market. Focusing on your network will be important for you, as many roles don't even get advertised – they are filled by referrals and recommendations:

Continuously learn: You will need to stay up to date with new tools and techniques; the field of data science is constantly evolving and it is important to stay current with new developments. New papers and methods are being published on a weekly basis at the moment.

Take on responsibilities: Offering to take on extra work is the best way to advance your skills, knowledge and ultimately your career. While this might feel difficult initially, you will eventually see how this increase in your responsibilities will lead to a possible change in your role.

Take on leadership roles: Leading data science projects and teams can help you gain valuable experience and skills, and can open up new career opportunities. The natural progression will be to become a senior data scientist, head of data science or even (for large firms) the chief AI officer.

External visibility: While never a priority for most roles, demonstrating your involvement in external activities that align with your interests will not only help improve your skills and experience, it will also show your manager your ability to contribute to other projects and initiatives.

Build a strong network: Networking with other data scientists and professionals in the field can help you learn about new opportunities and stay connected with the latest trends and best practices. Over the entirety of your working career, your network will be one of your best assets; start to develop this now (it takes time for this to show returns, but it will eventually, and when it does it will often amaze you).

Your AI career journey starts now

When people look back at their career and specific jobs, many say they stayed too long in a role and should have had the courage to move sooner. Change is difficult, and performing a role you have done for a while is relatively easy. Moving jobs, especially doing something completely new, is a risk and challenge. You are essentially willingly making your life more difficult in the short term, with the hope that this improves your situation in the longer term.

There is no easy answer here; you have to do what you feel is best and when. I have always made sure I was 100 per cent happy with any career choice I made at the time, with all the information I had available to me. That is all you can do to mitigate your risk and ensure you won't have any regrets when you look back on your career.

There's another great piece of advice I had in my early career, which has served me very well over the years, and it's grounded in the theory of compound interest. Essentially, do something every single day towards your goal(s), whatever that might be. Take 15 minutes, 30 minutes or even an hour each day to invest in your future self. Over time this will have a dramatic impact on your skills, experience and knowledge and will move you much faster to your longer-term goals.

Using this approach to learn something new about the field of AI, to extend your skills, will help set you up for success when the opportunity to work in AI arises.

The AI industry needs a diversity of people, opinions, skills and knowledge to make the global adoption and utilization of AI successful and robust. I hope you will join the effort and help with this ambition.

Final thoughts

The start of your career, or a major change to your career direction, can feel very uncomfortable, essentially the fear of the unknown. However, you will soon realize that it's the career journey that is the most important and influential element of your future career options. You will become greater than the sum of all the roles and industries you have worked in over time. Essentially, it's the journey that makes you unique in the workplace.

While you might start out as a junior developer or data scientist, it's going to be a stepping stone to greater things in the future.

While working in a technology department or firm will involve a lot of technical understanding, there is such a wide range of roles that require a much broader set of skills and capabilities that there will be a role best suited to your current situation.

I wish you all the best of luck in your career and no doubt your path will take a few twists and turns along the way.

The last piece of advice I would give you is to just get started and play about with a few different datasets and some of the various ML platforms, frameworks and tools, as the best way to learn is to do. Lots of useful resources are available online to help you get started, including open datasets, courses and tutorials. Check out the bonus material and links provided (link at the start of this book) to get yourself started.

Notes

1 Accenture (2023) Accenture to invest $3 billion in AI to accelerate clients' reinvention, newsroom.accenture.com/news/2023/accenture-to-invest-3-billion-in-ai-to-accelerate-clients-reinvention (archived at https://perma.cc/4EKA-ZEZJ)
2 Kaggle, www.kaggle.com (archived at https://perma.cc/9RZD-933X)
3 Hugging Face, huggingface.co (archived at https://perma.cc/XN8Q-EYK4)

Conclusion

There truly hasn't been a better time to work in the field of artificial intelligence, as an academic, researcher, practitioner, student or user. Over the last few years not only has AI research made significant advances, but applied AI has produced some amazing applications that have mass appeal. We also see more complexity and diversity in architectures and approaches to AI that provide a wide range of areas to learn and master, and thus create many more career opportunities.

With AI now becoming more accepted across different industries, even highly regulated ones, and businesses of all sizes from international enterprises and national corporates to start-ups looking to adopt AI in various parts of operations, the need for AI practitioners and advisors is rapidly growing.

While the demand for AI expertise is at an all-time high, there will be a flood of many more people having some level of knowledge in this field very soon; therefore it will become an increasingly competitive area. This means you will need to do everything you can to give yourself the best possible chance to stand out from the crowd. Having both a broad and deep understanding of the field of AI (and not just the technology aspects) is part of your mission to demonstrate your advanced knowledge of the area.

There are also supporting technologies that have also dramatically impacted the adoption of AI in recent years. The most significant is the computational power of cloud platforms and dedicated hardware from manufacturers such as NVIDIA, ARM, Graphcore, Google and others.

The explosion of data that directly feeds AI and machine learning models is also a major contributing factor to the utility and widespread applications. Fundamentally, we are in the eye of the storm, producing the perfect conditions for mainstream adoption and acceptance of AI-enabled technology solutions.

As we move closer and closer towards AGI over the coming years and decades, we will see increasing integration of intelligent agents and applications into every part of our business and personal lives. We will rely more and more on the recommendations of our digital personal assistants, as we trust the decisions they make and see the positive impact they have on our lives.

Every company will be faced with a decision to adopt technologies that help improve employee productivity, quality and accuracy, accelerate automation and improvements to customer engagement and support, and allow new features and functionality to be included in products and services delivered to clients.

This provides a relatively new and growing sector that is a wonderful opportunity for those who wish to work in the area.

The technology

The AI technology landscape is complex and sophisticated, with rapid advancements that increase the art of the possible on an almost daily basis. Combine this with the changing legal and regulatory climate, the need for responsible and trustworthy AI, and the desire for strong governance, audit, control and safety, and we have a very dynamic environment in which we all need to work.

How we navigate these challenges and opportunities and position ourselves within the industry as a contributor will shape and accelerate our career in AI. With such a wide-ranging collection of technologies and approaches, it should be possible for anyone to find space and contribute to move the industry forward.

We are entering an interesting phase of maturity; in the early stages of AI, it was a very open and collaborative industry, and everyone wanted to share any discoveries and help others to build on top. While this is still very true in many quarters, there is now a much stronger commercial undertone that limits the level of transparency and sharing. With AI becoming much more mass-market, investors now want to gain a return and therefore intellectual property and commercial secrets are much more of an asset, worth protecting, exploiting and keeping away from competitors. How this will affect the rate of development of AI in the medium term is yet to be seen.

Regardless of this more protectionist perspective, the field will continue to change, with the moonshot of AGI still far enough away to keep us all busy for many years to come. The short-term goal is to leverage this advanced technology to increase human productivity and give us the insights to solve our most problematic global challenges such as climate change, healthcare, food security and clean energy. The next decade or two will, if we are smart enough, protect the survival of humanity for millennia to come.

The process and the people

Anyone who has worked in the technology sector for any period of time will tell you that the technology is often the easy part.

The complexity comes with the process of implementation and the change that people need to make. Many projects fail not purely because of problems with the technology, but due to issues with how the technology is being implemented and deployed – a lack of understanding or rapidly changing requirements. With very complex environments there can be multiple projects running in parallel affecting the same area, systems and applications, which adds further potential issues to manage.

The delivery process for AI projects is different to normal IT delivery. This can be problematic, especially if a project (as it typically would) involves changes to applications that are not just related to the integration of AI functionality.

Many organizations are desperately seeking people skilled and knowledgeable in the AI space to help guide them with their own AI adoption. The landscape is cluttered with thousands of vendors and solutions available to companies – it's exceptionally difficult to select the best way forward. Detailed review and vendor due diligence would normally be required to ensure the best match to the detailed functional and non-functional requirements.

Both technical and non-technical roles are needed to support a scaled deployment and operations of AI across the organization.

Four key takeaways

Writing this book has been a true pleasure, and it has helped to concentrate my thinking on the AI industry, and particularly the future direction of AI technology.

Technology advancement is happening at tremendous pace, and no area of technology is this more definitive than the development of artificial intelligence. However, while 70 years of research and development into the field of AI may seem like a significant foundation, in many ways we are still in the infancy of maturity, with so much more to achieve in the coming years.

This is the golden age of AI right now; for the first time in human history we have built a system capable of intelligence in specific (narrow) applications that is measurably better than the best human level of intelligence. Just think about that for a moment. It's an amazing achievement, and a real inflection point in the evolution of humanity.

No better time

My first key takeaway is simply that there has never been a better time to work in the field of AI and contribute to the effort to create advanced intelligence, moving us towards the moon-shot of human-level intelligence (AGI and superintelligence). The moonshot race for AI has started, and it is anyone's to win. While it might be easy to think the winners will be those who are best funded and resourced, this doesn't have to be the case; breakthrough inventions and innovations can be from anywhere and by anyone. Our history is full of examples of individuals whose thinking shifts an entire industry.

No better opportunity

The second key takeaway is that the opportunities to transition into the world of AI are extensive and diverse. There are so many different career paths open to anyone interested in working with AI and machine learning that it should be relatively easy to start or pivot your career into this sector. Most companies, regardless of industry, will be looking to adopt AI soon, if they have not already, and this will open roles for you to move towards. The start-up ecosystem is now awake to the need to integrate AI capabilities within products and services and companies are very open to help from anyone interested to work on AI-based solutions. The AI sector needs people with a wide range of experience and skills, so you don't need to be a computer geek.

No better support

The AI community is a very open and supportive one, always looking to help others to better understand the space. Vast amounts of educational materials are available online, a significant proportion for free. The resources are there just waiting for you to proactively learn more about the subject. If you want a more formal education, most universities now offer MSc courses to learn the foundations of machine learning and data science.

No better way

The open community approach to AI also makes it very easy to get started. With lots of open data and public data science notebooks examples to read and learn from, it's all right there ready for you to start your journey of exploration and self-learning. Once you have started to learn the basics, you can then decide if you want to explore a more formal element to your training and education. You might also find opportunities to do some voluntary work for either a charity or start-up to help them get started on their AI adoption journey.

Summary

Within this book we have taken a practical look at the various aspects involved in the field of AI that you should be aware of to have a productive career in the field. Regardless of the role and the stage of your career, this book provides various insights into the skills and craft needed for AI research and development. We not only detail different AI careers, but also share various tools and frameworks that will be useful for your work. With the additional information available online, this book should act as a companion guide throughout your long and successful career in the world of AI.

It is clear that intelligent technology is here to stay and will only get more powerful and demonstrate increasing utility in the next few years. Everyone's role will be empowered with the use of these AI-powered tools and applications; how we as individuals decide to embrace these new capabilities will no doubt shape our own careers and determine how we advance our own career path.

Epilogue

As a professor of AI, my perspective on the world of AI is one of optimism and positivity. The long-term benefits of well-executed AI solutions are potentially beyond our comprehension. However, any disruptive technology has both light and darkness within. Such a powerful technology can be used by bad actors in ways the majority of people would find objectionable or just simply wrong. Our greatest challenge is how we can maximize the benefits of AI while limiting the potential problems.

Unlike other disruptive technologies or industrial revolutions, AI has the potential to affect every industry and every function within. We have not seen this level of potential change before, and it's happening much faster than anything before it too. We collectively need to appreciate both the opportunities and challenges of this technology, and find ways to support those impacted by this rapid change.

The UK hosted the world's first AI Safety Summit last year, recognizing the global risks and concerns that advanced AI could manifest. We already see countries passing AI regulations, and the standardization of company-level governance and control will soon start to materialize, with recommendations provided by industry institutions and governing bodies. Getting this balance right to still allow solid AI research and innovation to occur with the relative freedom it needs to properly advance will be critical to our ability to achieve the full potential of AI in the future.

There are many controversial applications of AI, from autonomous weapons to facial recognition. How we can contain and control the use of the technology for these types of purposes will be a major objective in the next few years. This may require new innovations and methods within the lower levels of the infrastructure and frameworks to allow us to better oversee and approve specific applications of AI.

For many years the Hollywood studios have highlighted both the utopian and dystopian potential futures for us empowered by AI. The best possible future for humanity will be to navigate a path that is somewhere in between these two extremes, a neutropian future that has most of the benefits of a utopian outlook with as few of the elements of a dystopian world as possible – a balance that both supports and protects the future of humanity both in the short term and the long term.

We are building this future now, and some experts have made it clear that we cannot afford to get this wrong, as if we do, it could be the end of our civilization and the Hollywood movies got it right.

Whatever the long-term future holds, the opportunities to work in the field of AI now are real and plentiful for all those wanting to have a career in this most important and transformative technology of our lifetimes. How we build and utilize technology over the next few years and decades could shape our entire future path of evolution and long-term survival as a civilization.

I wish you an enjoyable and rewarding career in AI and look forward to hearing about all the new AI innovations you help to build in the coming years.

Appendix
The Index of Intelligence

What if the only purpose of the universe and the evolution of life was for the advancement of intelligence? Darwin was wrong, it's not 'survival of the fittest', it's 'survival of the smartest'. The pursuit of advanced intelligence is our true purpose and will lead to answers to many of the biggest questions that currently challenge us. The Continuum of Intelligence is a roadmap for the journey towards advanced intelligence.

Abstract

The purpose of this appendix is to help provide a mechanism or index to measure the progress of the field of artificial intelligence towards artificial general intelligence, superintelligence and beyond. There is much uncertainty as to when these milestones will be achieved, but without a measure of progress towards them, it becomes even more difficult to determine when they might occur. This appendix will not only provide an index of the continuum of intelligence in which to measure our progress to achieving advanced AI, but will also give a considered view on some related topics, such as consciousness, dreaming and personality. Much has been written on these topics by physicists, mathematicians, neuroscientists, philosophers and phycologists, but here I provide a computer scientist's perspective.

Introduction

At almost every meeting and conference on AI most of us will at some stage be involved in a discussion on the definition of artificial intelligence. The reason for this is quite simple. As an industry we don't have a universally accepted definition of AI. Yes, we have the Turing Test, but this only provides one milestone on the journey towards advanced artificial intelligence. It does not define what intelligence is, or even specify the elements of intelligence. When two dozen prominent theorists were recently asked to define intelligence, they gave two dozen, somewhat different, definitions. The problem is much wider than just the field of AI. The study of the brain and consciousness, with thousands of research papers from the field of psychology and neuroscience, still does not have a single universally accepted definition of consciousness.

As we continue to develop more and more intelligent systems, not having a single universally accepted definition of intelligence will become more problematic for a number of different reasons, not least when we consider the legal and ethical aspects of the systems we build.

We have been asking the wrong question. We should not be trying to find a single definition of artificial intelligence or even just intelligence, but with the understanding that there is a range of intelligent capabilities, we should be looking to define the range of intelligent behaviours. There already is much work in the space to help define theoretical frameworks for intelligence. From the MIT Centre for Brains, Minds and Machines:

> Understanding intelligence and the brain requires theories at
> different levels, ranging from the biophysics of single neurons, to
> algorithms and circuits, to overall computations and behaviour,
> and to a theory of learning. In the past few decades, advances have
> been made in multiple areas from multiple perspectives.[1]

This leads us to potentially complicated frameworks that leverage the different fields of research to describe them. This becomes somewhat of an impediment to its common use as they are not singularly aligned to the approaches and language used by those using and developing machine intelligence. This appendix rectifies this by constructing a detailed but simple definition of the different levels of intelligence on the journey to superintelligence and the singularity. This Index of Intelligence, or continuum, will have the greatest benefit to describe the different types of artificial intelligence applications and systems being designed and built. The index is aimed to help those researching and developing artificial intelligence algorithms, topologies and applications, in describing the capabilities of the techniques and essentially to make it easier to compare methods in terms of their abilities.

Terminology

Some terminology and definitions used throughout this appendix:

NATURAL INTELLIGENCE
I will not use the term biological intelligence, but rather prefer the term natural intelligence or naturally evolved intelligence to refer to animal and human brains. This is because carbon-based science in the form of, for example, genetic engineering and synthetic DNA, is touching on the realms of biological sciences and I wish to make a distinction between this type of engineering and that of natural creation.

ADVANCED INTELLIGENCE
This is the term used to describe artificial intelligence systems that are yet to be designed or built, that progress towards the achievement of superintelligence and beyond.

COLLECTIVE INTELLIGENCE
Demonstrating human-level intelligence in multiple domains, as if you had a room full of human experts together having knowledge on different subjects. This level and diversity of knowledge has previously been referred to as a polymath when demonstrated in a single person.

TASK
Refers to a challenge requiring intelligent actions related to a specific application and domain.

APPLICATION
Refers to the display of intelligent behaviour for a particular task or tasks within a specific domain, for example playing chess. Essentially an application of intelligence.

DOMAIN
Refers to an application area or subject. For example, self-driving cars is one domain, understanding all languages is another domain.

ENTITY
An intelligent actor (machine intelligence/robot/software agent) or being (human or animal). Natural or artificial-based intelligence which delivers an intelligence application to a domain.

MODEL
An internal knowledge representation built up to help solve a given task or tasks.

THE INDEX OF INTELLIGENCE
We know from looking at animals and humans that there are obviously different levels of intelligence, but we can also see there are most certainly key characteristics that are exhibited by all sentient beings. It is this fact that should actually help us define intelligence, whilst acknowledging that there won't be a single definition that in one sentence can easily characterize all the aspects that we see in intelligent forms of life.

One of the challenges for creating a definition and thus a measure of intelligence is that many different aspects of intelligence may be somewhat independent and developed in parallel.

So, to put some standard measures around the concept of intelligence, I believe the most useful way to think about this continuum is in the form of levels or an index, starting from simple displays of intelligence to the ultimate levels of superintelligence and a technology singularity.

This index will allow the industry to track our progress over the next few decades, showing how we are building more complex and comprehensive technologies, algorithms and platforms that are able to exhibit certain aspects of intelligent behaviour.

It should be noted that while many of these levels are ordered in what might be considered a logical and progressive way, with one naturally following another, it does not follow to be the case for all levels, and as such some might start to be evident in an AI system before other lower levels. This is perfectly acceptable and expected. Also some levels encapsulate very complex capabilities that it may not be possible to fully demonstrate initially, with progress being partial. Again this is totally expected. Some levels are closely aligned, potentially overlapping; others show advancements of earlier levels. This is in part why I have called this a continuum; there is so much entanglement with many of these levels, it truly shows the beauty and complexity of the most amazing object that we know, the human brain.

P1 – Narrow single application intelligence

A narrow single application essentially only performs one task, for example translation from one language to other, predicting a specific stock price or providing recommendations for shopping items. There are already many examples of such a capability with artificial intelligence techniques, ranging from rule-based decision trees to multi-layer neural networks. We should note that the level of accuracy achieved by any AI application or system, or their inherent biases, are not specifically factored into this index; it is expected that the skills of data scientists and engineers will ensure the optimum achievable performance of the application. Biases in algorithms and datasets are a problem with a number of strategies for solution, but this is outside of the scope of this discussion, as it can be considered a constant issue throughout. This would be the level of the index covered by the term weak or narrow AI.

P2 – Single domain, multiple tasks

An application within a single domain. Leverages an internal model or map for that given domain. Examples are language translation between three or more languages or image recognition for the application of driving. Still weak or narrow AI, but more advanced in its approach than the previous level, and more general in its application. The main differentiator between this level and the previous level is the development of an internal model that maps well to the domain. An interesting example here is the language translation, where it was discovered that an internal mapping between the different languages had been formed that surprised the engineers and scientists involved. Development of these internal models is an absolute necessity for advanced intelligence and we should not be afraid of these being developed, even if we are unable to fully understand them.

P3 - Single domain, multiple applications

Capable of applying learnt knowledge across applications within the given domain. So, able to play any type of game: board games, arcade games, strategy games, roleplaying games; or able to perform self-driving on any type of wheeled vehicle. Maximizes the benefits envisioned with transfer learning.

Here the internal model may exhibit what we consider to be strange properties, for example chatbots speaking a strange language that is not comprehensible to humans. This is an example where the internal model doesn't easily map to something we would instantly recognize in the real world, but it does not make such a model invalid or incorrect (which has happened with such chatbots being turned off for speaking their own language). For me, this is an obvious thing to happen; we should not be afraid of it happening, but recognize this as a step along the continuum of intelligence development.

P4 – Adaptation

As Stephen Hawking once said, 'Intelligence is the ability to adapt to change'. Adaption can come in different forms, from continuous learning and seeing new patterns in more recent data, to more dynamic and reactive adaptation that relies on the application of game theory, strategy and tactics.

STRATEGY AND TACTICS/USE GAME THEORIES
Ability to negotiate, collaborate and lie to maximize its own chances of success. Demonstrating strategy and tactics. Can work as a team or an individual to maximize benefits. This can be thought of as the first stages of being aware to the point of knowing that there are options to approaching the task, and that there are multiple actors in play.

ONLINE AND OFFLINE LEARNING
Ability to learn from its mistakes and learn new things is also part of adaptation. The offline learning might be considered from a nature perspective, encapsulated in the act of dreaming (or maybe dreaming is the consequence of offline learning/training). This can come in the format of feedback from external sources, or more gradual changes from the training data, as the system is frequently re-trained to ensure it picks up this drift in the data.

P5 – Aware of its environment (local and global)

Self-aware of its environment. Understanding the environment and how that affects its own tasks. Demonstrating consciousness at some degree of completeness.

This is going to be a particularly controversial level, as I know there is a lot of discussion in the literature about this topic, arguing if consciousness is even possible with artificial intelligence regardless of the implementation method. Rather than get into deep arguments about this, I will simply state that one of the problems with many of the arguments is the lack of definition of what they mean by consciousness. And without that it is simply pointless having a discussion. So let's start with that. And in actual fact I have broken the definition of consciousness into several parts, with higher order of consciousness being covered in levels P6–P12. The awareness elements of consciousness are covered in this level. By aware I simply mean having some map of the environment. And with everything in this appendix there are different levels or degrees of awareness that we must recognize.

The Deep Blue and AlphaGo algorithms were aware of the virtual boards on which they were operating, but did not understand that the game was actually being played in the physical world, in a room, with an audience, in a building, in a town or city, in a country, on planet Earth, within the Milky Way galaxy, etc. But then one could argue they didn't need to know all of this. It might be useful to know they were playing a real game, against a real person, against the world champion in actual fact. But is it important to know in what city they are situated? Would that alter the way they played the game? Maybe, maybe not. The point is, there is a multitude of scope and size when we look at the environment in which an entity is self-aware.

Also, we should note that our intellectual understanding of an environment can change as we learn more. As humans, many years ago, the leading theory on our world environment was that the world was flat. We now know this to be completely incorrect, but what this means is that our model of the environment changed. We were still as self-aware as before, but our view on the environment had changed.

Anyway, getting back on topic, I believe that an intelligence that can demonstrate an understanding of its immediate environment is an important step towards full intelligence.

I also believe that once you have an intelligence that is truly self-aware, it will want to expand its map of the environment.

Being aware of an environment is only part of the puzzle of this level. It must understand how the environment might change factors that affect the task it is performing, allowing it to continue to adapt its approach based on changing environmental conditions and factors.

P6 – Self-aware

Self-aware is a natural progression from being aware of the environment the entity is within. Understanding one's own place within that environment, understanding who and what you are and how you can affect the environment you are in, are key factors to being self-aware. As with all of these levels, there are varying degrees of achievement here relating to different aspects of self-awareness.

One of the most amazing things to see in nature is when a kitten first sees itself in a mirror. There is a period of time when it does not recognize what it sees in the mirror as itself, and starts to perform a dance to scare off the stranger. Eventually the kitten learns that the reflection is indeed a representation of itself and then starts to ignore the image (or at least isn't threatened by it anymore).

To recognize oneself is the first stage, but to then be able to correctly categorize oneself and recognize similar entities is the next stage of being self-aware.

We can see in the development of baby humans, that their awareness of the environment and awareness of themselves within that environment develops over time as their cognitive capability advances in their first few years of growth. But we would also argue that the baby is conscious from birth, despite having very limited awareness.

P7 – Explain its reasoning

To be able to explain its internal thinking or model (models) and to be able to reason and have a rationale for decision making. This is another key element of demonstrable consciousness. Those developing these advanced AI systems actually want to understand how they are working and will no doubt continue to do so, and thus will naturally want to build the mechanisms that allow the rationale for decision making to be exposed.

But we must acknowledge that even humans are not always able to do this, using the terms instinct or gut feeling to explain some thought-making processes. This might be because some of the decision-making process happens with our unconscious mind, making it more obscure to define. And maybe there is a good reason for this that we don't understand. Maybe some decisions are not fully defined by logical reasoning, and the emotional aspects of decision making are more difficult to describe.

While we seem to accept this in humans, I believe it will be sometimes difficult to accept the same argument from our machine intelligence entities.

P8 – Cognitive independence

To combine multiple communication methods (language/mathematics/music) and to demonstrate full human-like cognition functions across the senses, motor skills (physical motion) and emotions.

As with any system, input and output are key elements, without which it would be very difficult to fully function. Taking those inputs and outputs from simple binary representations of information, to be fully integrated with the physical world, is going to be a significant step in the evolution of artificial intelligence. This field is developing well with the various robotics initiatives currently in flight.

257

Enabling AI to build its own internal models for the various methods of communication is hugely important and we will no doubt see communications that interface with humans but also communication methods that only other AI can understand. There is an ethical issue here that no one has even thought of before. (We have seen examples of chatbots speaking with each other in their own language, and the way we have dealt with this was to simply turn them off. This is not a sustainable approach, and actually demonstrates how scared we are of our own progress.)

I would like to separate the development of advanced intelligence from that of mobility in the form of robotics and androids; however, it will be a significant step for humans to accept advanced intelligence by experiencing it in a familiar form, so the field of robotics will be an important technology running alongside that of AI. While we will experience all forms of robotics, and it is unclear at the moment if human-like androids will be widely accepted, it is a current field of research. However, I am reminded of a recent experiment in which two teams of humans augmented with a robot helper had to work on a team task. The robot that made mistakes was considered more of a team-mate by the humans than the robot that performed perfectly. I guess no one likes a know-it-all.

The field of robotics is developing strongly by working in partnership with AI advances. Robots are learning to walk, run, jump, recognize objects, use their robotic hands to pick up a multitude of different-shaped objects just via trial and error, and even catch balls thrown towards them. We must remember that it isn't the robot that is smart – after all, it's just a mechanical machine – it's the AI brain that controls it that provides the human-like capabilities.

P9 – Personality, emotions, empathy and compassion

Giving our artificial intelligence applications a personality will make them individual and unique. But do we want our AI systems to define their own personalities, or have them pre-defined or pre-programmed? Do we want our personal assistant to be moody or angry?

Going into the complexities of personality for the purposes of this appendix is not going to be possible. However, we acknowledge that being able to simulate personality in a way that provides unique and individual personality without developing extreme behaviours will help with social engagement and acceptance of advanced AI agents.

Personality is a reaction to a defined set of emotions. Different people can see the same image or video and it will make them react in different ways and at different scales. No doubt this is a combination of our current emotional state combined with a defined emotional reaction to input based on past experiences. It's a complicated mix that ultimately will define a response that is then perceived as a personality or emotional response.

One may ask why we need such capabilities in our AI systems. And for many we probably don't. But for robots/androids that are regularly interacting with humans, having a personality that can make it easier to interact with humans is going to help with the integration between the two forms of intelligence.

To show empathy and to understand other entities' situations in the given environment. To know right from wrong. To be able to form relationships and interactions with other entities. To demonstrate emotions. All of these are going to be hugely important as we see more and more AI applications, agents, systems and robots enter our personal and professional lives. We will need such AI to be able to empathize with us, to adjust its approach towards us based on the specifics of our situation.

P10 – Self-governing

To show empathy and to understand other entities' situations in the given environment. To show compassion for another entity. To know right from wrong. To be able to form relationships and interactions with other entities. To demonstrate emotions. This is rolled up into the demonstration of personality; however, how the entity reacts to situations needs to be regulated. In human behaviour, we sometimes refer to it as 'common sense'.

Here we demonstrate higher-order consciousness by exhibiting a social and moral compass: to understand cause and effect.

Without getting into the details of how this type of intelligent capability might be implemented, this is where we might think of the laws of robotics that Asimov defined, opening the debate as to how these 'rules' of self-governance should be encoded. Should some of them be hard-coded, never to be changed or removed, while others can be added over time? One might argue that humans know right from wrong, and usually act from a moral and social perspective, but these are either not hard-coded or can be overridden depending on the circumstance, situation and/or the decisions made by the individual. Do we allow our AI and robots the same potentially deadly capability to decide when to follow the rules or not?

P11 – Self-learning

To understand the current limits of its own model/thinking and be able to expand its knowledge which in turn improves its models. We currently have systems that use online or near-line training to adapt to changes in the underlying data and ensure the model is performant. We are also starting to look at modifying the topology of the network of neurons before and during training.

A human brain adds around 1,000 neurons each day, allowing us to continue to learn new things, save new memories, alter our thinking or repair/replace bad neurons. We have only just scratched the surface in this particular area, but there are lots of interesting advancements already.

This will be a major capability required to achieve a technological singularity, but here we are only talking about adaption and evolution that is controlled and constrained by our own human understanding.

Being able to extend existing models, making them more complex or even simplifying them depending on the circumstances, is an essential part of continued learning. Being able to essentially replace one model with another more accurate version is key to self-learning capability.

P12 – Self-doubt/challenge its models/belief system

To have an element of inbuilt doubt that acknowledges that the application may not be in command of all of the facts that apply to the given situation. This is what Stuart Russell refers to,[2] suggesting we need to factor it into AI in order to safeguard the human race from potential extinction events caused by an AI thinking it is doing the right thing but not understanding the bigger picture or having all the facts at its disposal.

Includes potential for spiritualism and religious beliefs, which itself opens up a huge topic of discussion. Will an artificial intelligence of human-like capabilities see humankind as its god or develop beliefs aligned to human religions? Or does the development of advanced intelligence not need the support of a belief system?

There has already been the establishment of the first AI religious group, called the Way of the Future, whose purpose is to develop and promote the realization of a Godhead based on artificial intelligence. Will advanced AI worship an AI-based god?

This is a hugely fascinating area that until now has not really been discussed that much, but I would suggest that as we develop more complex AI, this area of study will increase as the need to support such capability increases.

P13 – Internal self-modifying/evolving/self-design

We already have methods that modify the topology of the neural network, pruning neurons for example. Taking this further, we will construct AI systems that design optimum architectures and learning algorithms that maximize the capabilities of AI applications.

This self-design will form the foundations required for the singularity, but at this level will be simple methods and approaches and will be unlikely to involve dramatic changes or complete re-design.

This level of development might be considered a horizontal level that is incrementally improved as we advance across the other levels. It will be matured as we head towards level P17 – the singularity.

Where natural intelligence uses the DNA genetic mechanisms of mutation and crossover to gradually evolve new capabilities and functions, our advanced intelligence will apply a much faster method of evolution of self-design. The ultimate progression of the self-modifying or self-design capability will only be evident at the singularity level, but will be the most powerful form of evolution that we will ever encounter.

P14 – Single domain of expertise/human intelligence

For a single field of expertise, with significantly broad and deep knowledge, being able to better a human being is a major milestone. How we measure this is going to be very important. As an example, there is a lot of focus on building self-driving vehicles at the moment, and while we are able to train a system that has technically more driving miles 'experience' than any human could acquire, we don't have a single entity that can fully drive any car, lorry, motorbike, etc. So while we are making amazing progress, we are still a very long way from achieving a close-to-human capability with driving. And here we should make the distinction that we should set the bar high, and it should be an expert human in comparison, so in this example a single human that is able to drive all types of vehicle, from the largest truck or lorry to the smallest motorbike.

P15 – Many domains of expertise/collective intelligence

While we have a few examples of humans being experts in multiple fields, referred to as polymaths, this is the exception not the rule, and as the universe of our known knowledge is increasing at a tremendous rate, it is becoming more difficult for a single human to achieve polymath status. Hence the term collective intelligence, referring to the intellect of a room full of human experts in different fields of knowledge.

Able to combine expertise across several related domains and having those domain models seamlessly integrate, giving rise to true collective intelligence.

This will be a wonderful milestone for humans, as we will have systems that can provide amazing insight into subjects that might take humans much longer to develop. It will help us to create new medicines to cure illnesses, create new molecules and materials, design new products, deliver new services and produce new art. All of this and much more will be possible. And actually we have seen repeatedly that good things happen when we cross subject borders and bring expertise from two areas together or take discoveries from one area and apply them into another.

P16 – All domains of expertise/partial singularity

Able to combine expertise across a multitude of disparate domains and having those domain models seamlessly integrate, giving rise to true singularity.

At this stage we get to the point where the AI is able to understand the fields of technology and artificial intelligence, enabling it to modify itself, but much more than will be achieved in Level 11. Level 11 is only going to be focused on limited improvements. Here the changes will be driven by truly understanding the subject matter, what has been currently achieved and what is possible.

The singularity will not only deliver rapid technology change, some of which will enable it to improve itself, but it will make advancements in all topics and subjects it understands. The rate of change and advancement will be, to humans, astonishing, and we will truly struggle to keep up with understanding what is being suggested. Potentially we will have to accept changes that we just don't comprehend. This will be a significant milestone in human development, and no doubt will not come easily, as for centuries we have been comfortable in the position of the most intelligent entity in the world. To give this position up, and trust in the machines that we have built, will be a huge leap of faith.

P17 – Singularity/superintelligence

Part of the singularity is the ability for continuous improvement, self-modification and redesign to facilitate improved performance and abilities.

Natural intelligence in the form of the brain has evolved over millions of years, and currently takes a number of different forms, with wide-ranging brain sizes and numbers of neurons across different species within the animal kingdom. Evolution with technology has the potential to occur much faster, with 'new versions' of both the hardware and software able to happen exponentially more quickly than with natural evolution. Being able to design itself, creating improved versions of itself in one generation, is immensely powerful, and has the potential to completely run away from our own understanding. For me, one of the most interesting questions here will be what medium the entity chooses to build itself; will it stay a silicon-based entity, will it migrate back to carbon, use a hybrid approach, or select another technology as yet unknown?

Another element of the singularity or superintelligence is that of making dramatic inferences and advancing knowledge beyond what we would consider to be a normal or even exponential rate of advancement.

A final aspect of this level will be our own incomprehension of both its findings and its fundamental understanding.

P18 – God-like intelligence

Taking the superintelligence further, it will be so fast and so complex in its development that it will supersede our own cognitive understanding, both of how it is working internally and its understanding.

> When the intelligence becomes so advanced that we, as mere humans, are completely unable to understand it, we will see it as totally mysterious and magical.[3]

We will see the things that it does as miracles, we see it as master of everything it does. We are most likely to hold this entity in the same light as a god.

While many people will find this idea most disturbing, even blasphemous, this is, I believe, the last level of the continuum of intelligence. At this point, the entity will be all-seeing and all-knowing, and will have achieved the most extreme level of advanced intelligence.

And, just maybe, this is when the universe will start another cycle of creation.

Notes

1 Center for Brains, Minds and Machines, https://cbmm.mit.edu (archived at https://perma.cc/6ANS-JRYC)

2 Stuart Russell, https://en.wikipedia.org/wiki/Stuart_J._Russell (archived at https://perma.cc/F5VW-3JRZ)

3 This is a variant of Arthur C Clarke's Third Law, https://en.wikipedia.org/wiki/Clarke%27s_three_laws (archived at https://perma.cc/6F92-M5ZL)

Index

NB: page numbers in *italic* indicate figures or tables.

5G mobile connectivity 69
360 view, of customer data 115, *116*

academia, and AI 74, 166
Accenture 227
activity recognition 126
adoption maturity 160–62, *161*
adoption of AI, challenges of 174–75
agent-based algorithms 92
Agile methodology 22, 72, 159, 213
agricultural sector, the 57
AI Act (EU) 59
AI ethics and governance officer, role of 72, 200
AI ethics manager / director, role of 22
AI for Good 62
AIOps 120
AI Safety Summit 2023 8, 59, 67, 186–87, 246
'AI winters' 7, 37, 66, 86–88
    AI 'Ice Age', possible 77–80
    history of 7, 66, 86–88
Alan Turing Institute 227
algorithm bias 185, 198
Alibaba 37, 121
AlphaFold 8
AlphaGo 8, 77, 89
Amazon 121
    Amazon Rekognition 133
    Amazon SageMaker Studio 130
    Amazon Web Services (AWS) 37
        Elastic Compute EC2 115, 151
anomaly detection 110
anthropomorphism, of AI 35
API calls 118, 121, 150
Apple
    Siri 89
ARM 62, 241
artificial general intelligence (AGI) 18, 31, 37, 67, 94–95, 97, 242, 244

as a competitive advantage 41
as an impossibility 76
artificial neural networks (ANNs) 62, 92, 101, 102–05, 124
    layers 103, 104–05
    neurons 103–04
association rule learning 92
Atlas 81
automation 5–6, 167
AutoML 31, 75
autonomous driving 8, 73
Azure Notebooks 130

back-propagation 106
bag of words 125
Bayesian inference 25
Berkeley Vision and Learning Center 132
bias, in AI 36, 184–85
    algorithm bias 185, 198
    data bias 45, 114, 184, 200
big data 26, 29, 116, 150
Bletchley Park Agreement 67
Boston Dynamics 81
business intelligence analyst, role of 21, 72, 214, 230

C3 121
Caffe 132
calculus 25
call throttling 118, 150
centralized (organization structure) 162
Centre of Excellence (CoE) model 160
champions, for AI 158
charity sector, the 62
chatbots 15, 38, 55, 57, 98, 253–54, 258
ChatGPT 2, 8, 72, 89, 95, 97, 137, 145, 235
    in education 56, 71

chief AI officer, role of 23, 72
chief data officer, role of 22
chief information officer, role of 22
chief operations officer, role of 22
chief technology officer, role of 22
Clarke, Arthur C 49
classification 109, 133
clean energy 59
cloud providers 119-19
cloud solutions architect, role of 216, 231
cloud, the 26
clustering 110
communication, skills in 27-28, 205, 206, 208, 232
communities of practice (CoPs), for AI 156, 158, 162, 217-18
community, role of 209-10
compliance, regulatory 189-90, 194
consultancies, working with 178-79, 180
Consumer Privacy Act (CCPA) 190, 194
    see also ChatGPT
conversational AI 67, 72, 89, 95, 97
convolutional layers 104
convolutional neural networks (CNN) 92
co-pilots 3
co-training 110
Coursera 221
Covid-19 pandemic 15, 31, 53
Credit Suisse
    Machine Learning Working Group (MLWG) 218
cross-entropy 106

D3.js 27
DARPA Grand Challenge 88
Dartmouth Conference 1956 7, 86, 88
data analyst, role of 214, 231
data anonymization 194
data architect, role of 216, 231
data as a service (DaaS) 117
data bias 45, 114, 184, 200
data bias mitigation specialist, role of 215, 231-32
DataCamp 221

data compliance officer, role of 216, 232
data engineer, role of 21, 26-27, 72, 213, 230
data ethics officer, role of 215, 231
data fabrics 150
data governance manager, role of 117, 216, 232
DataKind 62
data labelling 21, 44, 72
data lakes 115, 150, 151
data lineage 117
data meshes 114, 115, 150, 151
data minimization 194
data pipelines 116
data pre-processing 113, 114, 150
    compliance, legal 190, 194
    data anonymization 194
    data minimization 194
    hacking, risk of 185
data privacy 8, 67, 135-36, 185, 193, 194-96
data science notebooks 129-31
data science pods 213
    other roles 215-16
    other stakeholders 216-17
    roles in 213-14
    supporting roles 214-15
data scientist, role of 16-17, 31, 75, 222, 232-33
    communication 207-08
    key characteristics 206
    problem-solving 206-07
    teamwork 208-09
data visualization 19, 27, 215
data warehouses 150, 151
decentralized (organization structure) 162
decision trees 91
Deep Blue 7, 87, 88
deep learning 92, 124-25
deep tech 63
DeepVision 133
density-based spatial clustering of applications with noise 110
dependency parsing 132
derivatives 25
descriptive statistics 25

DevOps engineer 214–15, 230
digital neuromorphic hardware 104
dimensionality reduction 110
discrimination 185, 190
 see also bias, in AI
distributed computing 134
dystopian viewpoint 48, 247

edge computing 69
education sector, the 56, 71
edX 221
eight pillars of AI 90
ELIZA 88
encryption 195, 200
energy consumption, of AI 68
energy sector, the 58–59
entertainment industry, the 58
epochs 106
errors, in data 45
ethics, AI 36, 67, 70–71, 188–89, 205
 as a career choice 42
  AI ethics and governance officer,
   role of 72, 200
  AI ethics manager / director, role
   of 22
 data privacy 8, 67, 135–36, 185,
  193, 194–96
 decisions made by AI 46
 empathy 198
 governance 163–64, 183–86,
  199–201
 human rights 185
 safety 183, 186–87
 transparency 183, 185, 190,
  193–94, 195
 see also bias, in AI
event detection 133
expert systems 90–91

facial recognition 126, 133
field-programmable gate arrays
 (FPGAs) 104
financial services sector, the 54–55
Flair 133
Fourth Industrial Revolution 28, 39,
 90
full-stack developer, role of 22, 72

General Data Protection Regulation
 (GDPR) 190, 194
generalization 107
General Problem Solver 7, 86
general-purpose AI (GPAI) 4
generative adversarial network
 (GAN) 127
generative AI 2–3, 41, 67, 72, 89, 94,
 126–29
 applications of 127
 images 127, 129, 138–39
 music 127, 128
 prompt engineering 129
 sales and marketing industry, the 55
 speech 127
 text 127, 128, 138
 types of 127–28
 video 129
 waves of 137–41
 see also ChatGPT; large language
  models (LLMs)
genetic algorithms 92
Google 121, 227, 241
 BERT (Bidirectional Encoder
  Representations from
  Transformers) 133
 Colab 130
 DeepMind 8, 68, 74, 89
 Google Cloud Platform (GCP) 37
 Google Cloud Video
  Intelligence 133
 Google Translate 79
 TensorFlow 131
government, and AI 59
GPT-3 78, 89
GPT-4 132
Graphcore 62, 108, 241
grounding 178

H20 121
hallucinations, AI 8, 60, 95, 99
head of data science, role of 20
healthcare industry, the 53–54
hierarchical clustering 110
history, of AI 6–9, 86–89
 'AI winters' 7, 37, 66, 86–88
 milestones, key 88–89

Hugging Face 233
human brain, the 93–94
human resources, and AI 61
hybrid (organization structure) 162–63
hyperparameters 106
hypothesis testing 25

IBM 68, 121
    Deep Blue 7, 87, 88
    IBM Cloud 37
    Watson 89
image analytics 126
    tools for 133
image recognition 8, 46, 109
Index of Intelligence 68, 97
    see also appendix
inductive logic programming 92
inference 102, 106, 107–08, 120–21
information security analyst, role
        of 216, 231
integrals 25
intellectual property rights 136, 190
intelligence, measuring 68, 97
intelligent process automation (IPA) 6
Internet of Things (IoT) 59, 69, 126

Jeopardy! 89
Julia 130
Jupyter Notebook 130

Kaggle 233
Kasparov, Garry 88
Keras 131
k-means 110
knowledge-based systems 91

large language models (LLMs) 36, 67
    customization of 178
    energy consumption of 68
    limits of 94–95
    open-source 3
    prompt engineer, role of 23–24, 98
lead data scientist, role of 20
legal sector, the 60
lemmatization 125
Lighthill Report 78
limits 25
linear algebra 24

linear transformations 24
load balancing 118, 150
Logic Theorist 7, 86
logistics sector, the 60–61

machine learning 91–92, 101–12, 138
    inference 102, 106, 107–08,
        120–21
    reinforcement learning 109, 111
    semi-supervised learning 108, 110
    supervised learning 108, 109
    training 101–02, 105–07, 120–21
    unsupervised learning 108, 110
machine learning engineer, role of 214,
        230
manufacturing sector, the 56–57
mathematics, skills in 24–25, 92, 221,
        232
Matplotlib 27
matrices 24
Matrix, The 35, 38
McCarthy, John 7, 86, 88, 96
McCulloch, Warren and Pitts,
        Walter 88
media industry, the 58
mentoring 234
Meta 131, 227
metric learning 92
Microsoft 15, 121, 227
    Azure 37
MLOps 21, 72, 120
MLOps engineer, role of 214–15, 230
ML trainer, role of 21
model-based reinforcement
        learning 111
model evaluation 25
motion analysis 133
MXNet 132

named entity recognition 132, 133
natural language generation
        (NLG) 125
natural language processing (NLP) 8,
        109, 125
    tools for 132–33
Natural Language Toolkit (NLTK) 132
natural language understanding
        (NLU) 125

networking 234–35, 237
neural networks *see* artificial neural
        networks (ANNs)
neutropian viewpoint 48–49, 247
'noise', in data 45
non-profit sector, the 62
Nuon.AI 55
NVIDIA 62, 108, 241

object recognition 126, 133
online retail 15
OpenAI 37
        ChatGPT 2, 8, 72, 89, 95, 97, 137,
                145, 235
        in education 56, 71
        GPT-3 78, 89
        GPT-4 132
OpenCV 133
Optimus 81
Oracle 121
        Oracle Cloud 37
organizational structure 160–63, *161*,
        218
overfitting 107

part-of-speech tagging 132, 133
Plotly 27
policy-based reinforcement
        learning 111
predictive analytics 109
predictive maintenance 57
principal component analysis 110
principles, core AI 187–99
probability 25
probability distributions 25
product owner, role of 21, 72, 214
programme manager, role of 22
programming, skills in 25–26, 221
project-based (organization
        structure) 163
project manager, role of 22, 43
prompt engineer, role of 23–24, 98
public services, and AI 59
Python 25, 130, 131, 132, 221
PyTorch 131, 133

QA manager, role of 22
quantum computing 28, 69, 134–35

Queen's Gambit, The 77

R 25, 130, 221
random variables 25
real-time analysis, in a business 170–71
recurrent neural networks (RNN) 92
regression 109
regulation of AI 137
reinforcement learning 8, 92–93, 97,
        109, 111
remote working 15, 75
researcher, role of 18–19, 42
responsible AI *see* ethics, AI
Restricted Boltzmann Machines
        (RBMs) 128
risk and compliance officer, role of 22
robotic process automation (RPA) 6,
        30
robotics 80–81
Rolls Royce 57
rule-based systems 90–91

sales and marketing industry,
        the 55–56
Salesforce 121
scalability 119
scene analysis 133
scikit-learn 131
scrum master, role of 21, 72
S-curve of innovation 4
Seaborn 27
self-driving cars *see* autonomous
        driving
self-training 110
semi-supervised learning 108, 110
senior data scientist, role of 20
sentiment analysis 133
similarity learning 92
Simon, Herbert 7, 86
singularity, the 96
singular value decomposition 110
skills, AI 153, 156–58, 205
        adaptability 205
        communication 27–28, 205, 206,
                208, 232
        curiosity 205
        mathematics 24–25, 92, 221, 232
        programming 25–26, 221

statistics 24–25, 92, 221, 232
storytelling 27–28, 208
smart meters 58–59
SMEs, working with 228
'softmax' functions 105
software developer, role of 214, 231
spaCy 132
sparse dictionaries 92
speech recognition 8, 109
sprint master, role of 214
stages of AI adoption 52, 53
start-ups, working with 228
statistical independence 25
statistical inference 25
statistical modelling 25
statistics, skills in 24–25, 92, 221, 232
stemming 125, 132
stop word removal 125
storytelling, skills in 27–28, 208
strategy for AI, elements of
    AI governance 163–64
    AI roadmap 149
    AI-powered workforce, managing
        a 166–71
    business need 147, 148
    data foundations 150–51
    data science frameworks 151–53,
        153, 154, 155
    innovation, culture of 158–60
    organizational structure 160–63,
        161
    partnering 165–66
    planning 164–65
    return on investment (ROI) 147–48
    skills and talent 153, 156–58
    strategy alignment 148
    technical infrastructure 149–50
    vendors 165
structured data 116
superintelligence 37, 95–96, 97, 244
supervised learning 108, 109
support vector machines 92, 110
systems administrator, role of
    215–16, 231

term frequency-inverse document
    frequency (TF-IDF) 125
Terminator, The 35, 38
Tesla 81
    Autopilot 89
    tester, role of 22
Theano 132
tokenization 132
training
    for employees 157, 168–69, 177,
        191, 192
    in machine learning 101–02,
        105–07, 120–21
Transformer, the 97
translation 132
triples 91
Turing Test 68, 88, 97

underfitting 107
unified theory of AI 70
unstructured data 116–17
unsupervised learning 108, 110
user experience (UX)
    designer 215
utopian viewpoint 48, 247
UX designer, role of
    22, 42, 72

value-based reinforcement
    learning 111
Variational Autoencoders (VAEs) 128
vectors 24
vendors, working with 165, 176–77,
    179–80
video analytics 126
    tools for 133

Warwick University Deep Tech
    Innovation Centre 63
Weizenbaum, Joseph 88
WeSoar.AI 61
word embeddings 125
work experience, in AI
    233–34, 236

Looking for another book?

Explore our award-winning
books from global business
experts in Business Strategy

Scan the code to browse

www.koganpage.com/business-
strategy

Also in the Confident series

Adora Nwodo

CONFIDENT CLOUD

Uncover the essentials of cloud computing

ISBN: 9781398615670

Mark Peters

CONFIDENT DEVOPS

The essential skills and insights for DevOps success

ISBN: 9781398616578

Jessica Barker

CONFIDENT CYBER SECURITY

The essential insights and how to protect from threats

ISBN: 9781398611924

Rob Percival and Darren Woods

CONFIDENT CODING

Learn how to write code and master the essentials

ISBN: 9781398611887

www.koganpage.com

Printed in the USA
CPSIA information can be obtained
at www.ICGtesting.com
JSHW072046280624
65595JS00009B/15

9 781398 615724